Get in the Act!

60 Monologs, Dialogs and Skits for Teens

SHIRLEY ULLOM

MERIWETHER PUBLISHING LTD.
Colorado Springs, Colorado

Meriwether Publishing Ltd., Publisher
PO Box 7710
Colorado Springs, CO 80933-7710

Editor: Arthur L. Zapel
Cover design: Tom Myers

Printed in the United States of America
First Edition

Library of Congress Cataloging-in-Publication Data

Ullom, Shirley, 1938-
Get in the act! : sixty monologs, dialogs, and skits for teens / by Shirley Ullom. -- 1st ed.
p. cm.
ISBN-13: 978-1-56608-007-1
ISBN-10: 1-56608-007-X
1. Acting. 2. Dialogues. 3. Monologues. 4. Young adult drama, American. 5. Teenagers--Drama. I. Title.
PN2080.U44 1994
812'.04108--dc20 94-37678
CIP

4 5 6 07 08 09

For my two sons, their friends
and all the students
I've had through the years . . .
thanks for helping me
capture the teenage spirit!

CONTENTS

Monologs

M = Male *F = Female* *O = Optional*

Dialogs

M = Male *F = Female* *O = Optional*

Skits

M = Male *F = Female* *O = Optional*

M = Male *F = Female* *O = Optional*

PREFACE

In *Get in the Act!* I've tried to portray all the kids who've entered my classroom . . . touched my life. I've tried to hit on some topics that teenagers can't ignore — driving and drinking, elderly grandparents, teenage parties, smoking, broken homes, alcoholic parents and death.

I think the teenager is a strange phenomenon, and I've tried to explore his/her actions, problems, attitudes, lifestyle and humor in these monologs and skits. You kids are always "on-stage," so what better way to uncover some of your hidden secrets! Sure, I've had a great time poking fun at your weak spots, but I've also enjoyed playing up your strengths!

I've always worked with teenagers and found them to be honest, sincere, outspoken, insecure, outrageous, fearless and most of the time delightful. You'll find all of these traits portrayed by the characters in this book.

I hope *Get in the Act!* stirs up some awareness . . . and most of all I want teenagers to enjoy being my characters. (After all, where do you think I got them?) Puff some of your teenage breath into them . . . bring them to life . . . grab a little grease paint . . . a little limelight . . . and get in the act!

TIPS FROM THE AUTHOR

These writings are for you, kids. Feel free to change the names, locations, etc., as you see fit. And if some new "G-rated" slang words or phrases come along . . . add them! I can't do everything, you know!

Monologs

1

WHERE HAVE ALL THE PRINCE CHARMINGS GONE?

1 I often wish I lived in a fairy-tale world . . . in the Land of
2 Oz like Dorothy or in a far-off kingdom like Cinderella. How
3 delightful it would be to have a prince put a glass slipper on
4 my foot and make me a princess. The only guy who's ever come
5 near my foot is Freddy who stepped on my new Nikes with his
6 size fourteen hoof the first day of my junior year. Cindy and
7 Snow knew "someday their prince would come," but if a girl
8 expects one today she's going to need some kind of fairy
9 godmother! Believe me, the old gal'll need a wand that's pretty
10 potent . . . although changing today's guys into anything
11 resembling royalty *is* sort of like working with pumpkins! And
12 you know what they say about kissing a frog and having it turn
13 into a prince. Believe me I've tried this . . . these lips have
14 touched my share of toads . . . and after hours of lip locking,
15 I've seen no noticeable signs of nobility!
16 The only crown a guy wears nowadays is a Raiders' cap . . .
17 backwards. These modern-day Romeos would *never* stand
18 under a girl's balcony and say, "Oh, speak again, Bright Angel."
19 They might plunk a Garth Brooks tape in their tape deck and
20 hum along!
21 When it comes to manners, the average teenage male is
22 so handicapped he should be able to park in the front parkings
23 at the mall! He never heard of opening a car door; he belches
24 after he finishes his Big Mac, and he stares (or drools) at every
25 girl who goes by in a short skirt.
26 Why can't guys be more like my dad? Mom said he sent
27 her flowers, wrote her poetry, and brought little surprise gifts
28 for no reason. One guy did buy me a box of candy for Valentine's
29 Day . . . but all the caramels were missing.
30 My girlfriends and I are waiting for someone like Richard
31 Gere to swoop us away like he did in "An Officer and a
32 Gentleman." We want the romance . . . the fairy tale. Are there

1 **any Rhett Butlers out there?**
2 **I really think the reason guys aren't more romantic is that**
3 **their heads are too full of other stuff. They are mostly concerned**
4 **about their bodies — the old biceps. They have been**
5 **"Rambotized"! They think the way to a girl's heart is through**
6 **muscle tone. They will pump iron for two hours and then be**
7 **too lazy to pick up their own socks. Being a macho stud is more**
8 **important than being a gentleman. Not that we girls don't**
9 **appreciate a guy with a good build . . . but we'd like a little**
10 **sensitivity, too.**
11 **We realize there are a few drawbacks to being a guy. We**
12 **know it must be tough sucking up all of his courage to ask a**
13 **girl out . . . when she might laugh in his face. Of course, some**
14 **of that indifference you fellas give off could just be a cover-up.**
15 **Maybe you're protecting your inner feelings from possible**
16 **rejection from me and my sharp-tongued fellow females. So,**
17 **knowing this, we say there's still hope for many of the teenage**
18 **male population . . . sure, they're still croaking a little right**
19 **now, but with a little effort (and perhaps some Right Guard**
20 **and Scope) some of today's teenage guys could turn into**
21 **tomorrow's Prince Charmings!**
22
23
24
25
26
27
28
29
30
31
32
33
34
35

2

THE DAY I BECAME A WOMAN

1 Most men can look back on their lives and point out their
2 biggest mistake — maybe they joined the army too young, chose
3 the wrong woman, didn't eat enough fiber, or had "Mommy"
4 tattooed on their thigh. I was not lucky enough to make one of
5 these simple mistakes . . . oh, no, I played the leading role in
6 our junior class play. What's wrong with that, you ask? Nothing,
7 if I had played a dastardly villain, a Texas cowboy, or a
8 Valentino lover, but you see, I played the *female lead*!
9 It was an accident. My mother did not raise her only son
10 to be a female impersonator. I had this great little character
11 part — learning the lines would not be too much stress on the
12 old brain cells . . . lots of cute, dramatic babes to hit on . . .
13 everything was going great! That is till Cindy, the female lead,
14 broke her leg in three places in a skiing accident at Winter Park.
15 Mr. Colman asked for a volunteer to read Cindy's part till
16 he could find a replacement. Being the "wise butt" that I used
17 to be, I volunteered since I was never on-stage with Cindy's
18 character, the middle-aged spinster, Ms. Hobblehip. I would
19 still have been OK, just looked upon as helping out, a
20 courageous stand-in, a guy with a terrific show-must-go-on
21 attitude. Now, remember the "wise butt" part? Here's where it
22 kicks in. I couldn't just *read* the part and take my bows. Oh,
23 no. I mustered up every bit of dramatic talent I possessed and
24 with a curly gray mop covering my Dumbo ears gave the
25 performance of my career . . . we're talking Oscar time here! I
26 got a standing ovation from the cast. Well, you can guess the
27 rest. The search for Ms. Hobblehip was over . . . and so were
28 my high school days of being a babe hound! The girls who used
29 to hang around me and flirt now wanted to paint my toenails!
30 The ones who used to share my popcorn in darkest corners of
31 Cinema II began bringing me support hose! They made a big
32 ceremony of shaving off my peach-fuzzed beard and plucking
33 over my nose where my eyebrows grew together like a whiskery

1 worm.
2 I know the *Tootsie* and *Mrs. Doubtfire* roles brought
3 nothing but awards and wealth to Dustin and Robin . . . but
4 believe me, the only thing I got for donning female
5 undergarments (I would have killed, by the way, for Mrs.
6 Doubtfire's padding) was blisters on my heels from wearing
7 librarian shoes, laughed out of the jocks' club, invited to join
8 the Daughters of the American Revolution, and a new nickname
9 — Hobblewobblebutt!
10 It's too late for me. I'll have to travel down dark alleys
11 wearing shades. But the rest of you fellows, heed this advice:
12 Never, I mean *never* play the part of a female . . . not even for
13 a joke. Once you wear Hanes Her Way and Playtex you lose
14 your manhood forever. I'll go to college in another
15 state . . . miles away from my famous three curtain calls. My
16 folks will have to pay out-of-state tuition, but they deserve it.
17 Mom thought it would be a "cute" part and Dad videoed it to
18 show at family reunions. Well, I'll catch you later. I've got to
19 go before the Boys Glee Club sees me and breaks out singing
20 "Pretty Woman"!
21
22
23
24
25
26
27
28
29
30
31
32
33
34
35

3

WE WON'T FORGET BOBBY

1 I'm glad it's over. What a ritual . . . I think funerals should
2 be outlawed, condemned, vetoed. People crying . . . saying nice
3 things about Bobby just because it's expected . . . people who
4 didn't even know him. How could they be sure he was a sweet
5 little kid? I know they meant well . . . and Mom did seem
6 comforted by the flowers and cards. I hated all of it . . . I want
7 Bobby back! *(Picks up picture.)*
8 He was only six years old . . . he wasn't through losing his
9 baby teeth. He'll never get to play baseball or go out for track.
10 He didn't even get to finish kindergarten . . . it's not fair! What
11 are all those hotshot doctors doing in those labs? They can't
12 even save a little kid with cancer.
13 It hurts to think what a good sport he was. He laughed at
14 his hair loss . . . his friend Billy shaved his head so Bobby
15 wouldn't feel so embarrassed. He never complained . . . even at
16 the end. He worried about Mom and Dad . . . yes, and even me,
17 the big sister who treated him like an unwanted pest. I never
18 did apologize for yelling at him every time he sneaked into my
19 room and played with my teddy bears. I hope he knows I put
20 his favorite, Mr. Teddykins, in his arms before the services . . .
21 so he won't have to make that long journey alone. That's my
22 way of saying I'm sorry, Bobby.
23 I didn't mean it, Bobby, when I said the folks liked you
24 best. I was just jealous when they brought a new baby home
25 and suddenly I was getting second billing. I told Mom I hated
26 you, but it wasn't true. I'd sneak into the nursery and rock
27 you . . . when you were already asleep. I was proud when you
28 took your first step . . . and called me "thissy"! You were special
29 to me, Bobby. Now you're an angel . . . God sure knows how to
30 pick them!
31 Well, I've got to go help Mom pack up your clothes for the
32 Salvation Army. Mom and I hate to part with any of your stuff,
33 but there are kids out there who really need jeans and shirts.

1 Don't worry, I'm keeping your Bronco shirt and your Tweety
2 Bird sweater . . . someday my own little "Bobby" will wear
3 them.
4 Mom's afraid we'll all forget you, Bobby. But that will
5 never happen. Do we forget about the flowers when the ground
6 is covered with ice and snow? Do we forget about a spring rain
7 after the sun comes out . . . or the sunset at the break of dawn?
8 Your image is etched so deeply in my heart, Bobby, I'll
9 remember every detail. Your life was short, but you brought
10 so much joy to everyone, especially your family. And remember,
11 Bobby, wherever you are, someone down here loves you very
12 much . . . and that someone is your big "thissy."
13
14
15
16
17
18
19
20
21
22
23
24
25
26
27
28
29
30
31
32
33
34
35

4

VACATION FROM HELL

If you've never been on a family outing . . . a chance for parents and children to spend a little quality time shut up in an air-tight Buick . . . where everything from sleeping bags to Grandma is loaded in the trunk . . . and you *get* to travel eleven hours a day — *nonstop* (except for thirty-second refuels . . . and if your kidneys aren't in tune with the gas tank — *tough*) . . . If you haven't been fortunate enough to experience this special "family bonding," then you're one of the lucky ones!

Oh, sure, it sounds good when Mom brings out the Disneyland brochures . . . and who doesn't want to wade in the ocean and go deep sea fishing? But between our midwestern state and all this fun lies *many* bumpy, car-sick, tear-stained, argument-infested miles on the road! My father thinks he's Wyatt Earp behind the wheel of his new car . . . taking chances with the speed limit. My mom has to massage his neck because he's always getting it twisted to make sure a highway patrol car isn't clocking him. My sister whines all the way . . . her makeup is melting in the trunk, her boyfriend will find someone better the two weeks we're gone (if the jerk can't find someone better, he needs a brain transplant!). She worries that the California sun will dry out her skin or bleach her hair . . . she's bored, and her butt's numb! She's a real delight. To save my sanity and to keep Dad from kicking both of us out along some desert highway, Mom often lets me sit in front . . . in the suicide seat (the guy who named it must have known about my father's driving).

Then there's the food situation. Dad never wants to stop — "Burnin' daylight," he says in his John Wayne voice. But he also refuses to let us eat and crumb up his new speed machine. So, it's for sure we'll be malnourished by the time we hit the Sunshine State.

Entertainment on the road is nonexistent. The radio's a major problem in this family-run-away-from-home trip. Dad wants to hear country western ... Mom prefers classical or "golden oldies" ... I prefer something at least from the 90s, which Dad outlaws as obscene and causing moral decay and deafness in our youth! My sister has her own headphones — who knows what's happening between her ears! Also, Mom's mad because we all refuse to play the "cutesy" car games she's invented.

Finding a motel is another major hazard. Mom prefers to have advance reservations at reputable Best Westerns. Dad, who keeps reminding her he's paying the bills and calling the "stop" shots, prefers the old drive-till-we-drop method ... he doesn't want to be tied down to a certain motel or town when he might possibly have enough strength to make it another hundred miles. Don't worry that Mom's hanging out the window in exhaustion, I've swallowed half a bottle of Tylenol (some for a headache, some to fill the growling in my stomach), and my sister's filled three barf bags (eleven hours of family-filled fun seems to upset her delicate digestive tract). But I have to hand it to Dad ... he always stops at motels with swimming pools ... for the kiddies, he says. But, by the time we hog-tie, arm wrestle, plead and blackmail Dad into stopping, it's after ten o'clock and the pool's always closed.

So, all-in-all I can't say enough about family vacations. I know I can't wait till I grow up ... so I can be the driver ... choose the fun spots to drag my kids to. It's going to be great making others suffer the way I have ... getting my road revenge!

5

TEACHER'S PET: PIECE OF CAKE

It's easy to get on the good side of "any" teacher. I know, there are a few hard-nosed, lecture-giving, homework-hungry chalkdusters who seem to be rounded . . . and have no good side! But, believe it or not, even those pain-in-the-buns professors can be "had" if you really work at it.

I didn't say it was going to be easy — losing your baby teeth wasn't easy . . . locking lips on your first date wasn't easy . . . interviewing for a job you didn't want but your dad wanted for you wasn't easy . . . so why would you expect that learning to be a major "kiss-up" would be easy? Now, for some of you it's going to come naturally. You were the lucky ones . . . born with a God-given talent for buttering up teachers. The rest of you *listen* and *learn*.

First and foremost, your conduct must be flawless. Save your wisecracks and class-clown act for gym. Once the teacher sees that you're a "model" student, start in on the old compliment trick. I know it's an old gimmick, but so are spit wads and paper airplanes and they're still flying. Now, here comes the hard part . . . don't gush and watch out for overkill. Teachers have built-in radar and can spot the obvious apple polisher quicker than they can tap your fingers with a ruler! Practice your "kiss-up" techniques with a tape recorder till you get the tone of the voice just right — somewhere between sincere and prayerful. Then study your victim for days before you drop your "trite tribute" at the professor's feet. Remember, teachers aren't stupid, so if her hair looks like leftover spaghetti, she's going to suspect something if you compliment her on her Cindy Crawford tresses. So, go easy . . . they can spot a phony phrase . . . safe bets are usually penmanship, voice, shoes (the sturdiness or comfort — forget style!) and maybe the occasional shirt or jewelry.

Another *must* is to find out the victim's birthday (sweet talking and a gift to the school secretary often gets you access to the teacher files . . . or she'll jot the important date down for you if your story's believable). On their special day, discreetly slip a meaningful card or, better yet, an original poem, on their desk before class. It's best not to let the rest of the class share your apple polishing! Classmates will either ridicule you or steal your techniques!

Another neat trick that often works is offering to help grade papers (getting to look at tests could come in handy in the future). Flowers from your garden soften most teachers' hearts. So does a little taste treat like chocolates on Valentine's Day or homemade candy at Christmas. If your family takes a little trip to the Ozarks or Universal Studios, bring teachers pencils or pens . . . they are cheap (often given as souvenirs) and they yield big dividends! Little tokens keep your name at the top of a teacher's list . . . and then she'll mention your sterling qualities in the teachers' lounge . . . and this will have a domino effect and before you know it you've become a legend . . . one of the "good" kids . . . the white hats! But Bill, the champion teacher-kisser-upper in our school, still says the thing that works best, since teachers are so underpaid, is to staple a ten dollar bill to every poorly prepared assignment!

There are lots of other sure-fire methods out there just waiting to be tried to win your way to a teacher's heart. OK, OK, I know most don't have hearts . . . but if you strain your creative soul, you'll be able to come up with a scheme that will make you the next teacher's pet!

6

DAYDREAMING

1 "I'm sorry, Ms. McGill. I'll pay attention. Yes, I'll quit my
2 daydreaming."
3 I'm in trouble again. It seems I'm always doing detention
4 for not listening in class. I don't blame Ms. McGill. She works
5 hard to teach us English; not like my history teacher who's too
6 lazy to get out of his chair, so he just says every day, "Outline
7 the next chapter." It's easy to daydream in his class, but I'll try
8 to pay attention in English. I *need* to know how to write if I'm
9 going to break away from this life that's so unbearable I have
10 to daydream to survive.
11 I guess I'll write my essay on my "fantasy" life. Ms. McGill
12 would flip if I told her the truth. She's probably never been in
13 a trailer park . . . or lived in a mobile home with seven other
14 people and two dogs. That's why my clothes look so crumpled
15 and my hair's never clean enough. The shower's been broken
16 for weeks, and it doesn't seem to bother anybody but me. That's
17 the good part about P.E. — plenty of soap and water. Mom
18 always says she'll get things fixed when the next welfare check
19 comes in, but she usually spends the money on a new outfit
20 and a carton of cigarettes for herself and three loaves of day-old
21 bread and a big jar of cheap peanut butter for us kids.
22 I know other kids have it a lot worse, so I'm not complaining.
23 Besides, I have hope. Grandma's coming through next month
24 and she told Mom if she wasn't taking good care of us kids, she
25 was taking us back to the farm in Iowa. Grandma has fresh
26 milk and eggs every day. She bakes her own bread — fresh.
27 None of that green mold on the edges. Mama says we'll have
28 to clean up this place good before Grandma gets here . . . she
29 means I'll have to clean it.
30 Well, got to get this paper done. There's no good lights or
31 writing area at home. I lost my math book last week . . . Kenny
32 dropped peanut butter on it and the dog ate it. It was hard
33 telling Mr. Felts the dog not only ate my paper but my book!

1 **Let's see . . . I'll write about my hobbies — needlepoint,**
2 **baking fancy cookies and horseback riding. If it was good**
3 **enough for Walter Mitty . . .**
4
5
6
7
8
9
10
11
12
13
14
15
16
17
18
19
20
21
22
23
24
25
26
27
28
29
30
31
32
33
34
35

7

KISS OFF THAT FIRST KISS

I hate dating. No, I'm *not* wierd, and I'm not trying to knock down the closet door. I just hate to date because of that first kiss! It's just so awkward . . . it's like the flu — you know it's coming and you know you're going to suffer, you just don't know *when.*

I really think a guy should just walk up to a strange girl he's attracted to and kiss her . . . yep, plant one right on her and get it over. Then, if she doesn't blacken his eye, use a knee lift that makes him sing soprano or call the cops, he should date her for the next eight years . . . because the hard part is over — *the first kiss*!

Each generation has faced this problem. Gramps said he would stretch his arms, let one fall on her shoulder . . . then the ear nibbles that would lead to the first lip-locking session. Dad said he grabbed Mom on the porch swing and it was so dark he got her chin on the first try. (It's such a problem a guy almost needs target practice!)

My friend Kyle has a long nose and is always sticking it in the girl's eye. Kenny wears braces and has done his share of lip damage. Then there's always the question: open or closed lips? And length of time: do you hang in there till you run out of breath and the girl hyperventilates, or do you peck and run? There's a manual to drive a car, operate a computer, fix a flat tire; videos on how to improve your golf swing, trim down your waist, invest your money; but no help out there anywhere on how to give that all-important first kiss!

So, you're on your own, fellas. There's no safety net . . . so just jump! And if you're lucky you'll land your lips on hers . . . and then you can go on and have a good time on your date . . . because you have that blasted first kiss out of the way!

8

TEACHERS: WHERE DO THEY GET THEM?

1 Did you ever wonder where the school board goes to get
2 such a weird bunch of teachers? Do they throw out large
3 butterfly nets? Perhaps they have a magnetic force that draws
4 them in from outer space. Or do they interview at state mental
5 hospitals? Wherever they find these chalk-dust carriers, I wish
6 they'd buy round-trip tickets . . . so we could send them back!
7 It's not that these professors lack a certain amount of
8 intelligence. No, for the most part they have a fair amount of
9 gray matter; it's those strange, *Twilight Zone* personalities
10 (those little irritating quirks) that make us write four-letter
11 words about them in our textbooks and decorate the restroom
12 walls with obscene drawings of their "bloated" bodies. It's my
13 guess that Stephen King got the inspiration for his characters
14 from the faculty pages of his high school yearbook. Where else,
15 excluding the mug shot books at the police station, could one
16 find such an array of sad misfits?
17 Take my old math teacher, Ms. Wollygoogen. She has these
18 huge rolls of fat around her waist that jiggle when she's putting
19 fractions on the board. We can't concentrate on the math
20 because we're too busy watching her bowl-full-of-jelly belly do
21 the wave! It doesn't take much to distract the average teenage
22 mind.
23 And we don't stand a chance to learn anything in
24 chemistry because our teacher, Mr. Collins, is a fire-breathing
25 dragon. Really! His breath smells like he's been licking an
26 ashtray, and when he bellows out the Periodic Table of the
27 Elements we all suffer from nicotine poisoning. So you really
28 can't blame us for our low grades in science.
29 Now, Ms. O'Neal is another kind of distraction. She has
30 the body of Wonder Woman that turns the girls into jealous
31 felines and the guys into drooling androids. So scratch high
32 academic achievement in French.
33 Mr. Peters, the art teacher, is just a basket case, and Mr.

O'Conner the drama coach we suspect is a cross dresser. And nobody since Shakespeare's time has ever had a sane English teacher. I ask you: would a normal person with both oars in the water (or even in the boat) dedicate his/her life to conjugating verbs, undangling participles and quoting Elizabeth Barrett Browning?

Now where, I ask you, is the PTA, who won't let us have school activities on a church night or Coke with our lunches, when the school board does its hiring? Where is the Humane Society? We really aren't asking for much — just normal instructors . . . with a level head, kind heart and a terrific sense of humor. We're begging you — a mind is a terrible thing to waste . . . and we teens are losing it! Think about it . . . write editorials . . . I've gotta go now; I'm late to my world history class. Mr. Wadsworth (alias Mr. Foodaholic) is having us rebuild the pyramids out of marshmallows!

9

GRANDMA'S TRUNK

1 Have you ever lost someone you really love? I've lost my
2 grandma. No, she's not dead — not really; there's been no
3 funeral. But the funny, warm lady who helped me make May
4 baskets and banana muffins is no more. You see, Grandma has
5 Alzheimer's disease.
6 I really didn't know much about this awful illness till
7 Grandma started getting so forgetful, and it got worse — fast!
8 Now she doesn't know me at all — the granddaughter who was
9 born on her birthday, named after her. That really hurts.
10 There's nobody to talk to; Dad tries to forget about her. It's his
11 way of handling a bad situation — just pretend it doesn't exist.
12 He never goes to the rest home; he just says it doesn't do her
13 any good because she doesn't know him anyway. I go twice a
14 week, and tell her the stories she told me when I was four. She
15 loves nursery rhymes, and last week I took her my old teddy
16 bear (the one she gave me when I was two). She cried. But she
17 fell asleep with it cuddled up to her chest.
18 Even though my grandma is gone, I have something so
19 real to remember her by. You see, Grandma had this old, beat-
20 up trunk that was filled with her treasures. No, nothing that's
21 worth much in dollars and cents — but Grandma used to get
22 out her key on rainy afternoons and say, "Guess what? We're
23 going to open the trunk!"
24 I can't begin to tell you how excited I was. At each opening
25 Grandma would share some relic from years gone by . . . and
26 with it some story of her past. I saw her mother's purse — faded
27 but filled with coins, letters and studded combs for her hair.
28 Grandma always held the purse close to her lips before replacing
29 it in the trunk. I now have Grandma's purse, and I'm beginning
30 to feel the same emotion Grandma felt when she held her
31 mother's bag.
32 The trunk was filled with artwork. No, nothing that
33 belongs on a ceiling in a chapel . . . just simple valentines and

pictures drawn by childish hands and placed in a container for safe keeping by a loving mother's hand. I showed Dad some of his early artistic talents, but he just tossed them in the trash. I smoothed them out and put them back in their folder. My favorite "treasure" is the bundle of love letters written to Grandma by my grandfather, who died before I was born. He even wrote some light verse . . . I copied some of his poems for my literature notebook.

There is a tiny jewelry box in one corner. It contains some old brooches, hat pins and a cameo ring. Most of these belonged to my great grandmother. Grandma let me wear the ring sometimes when I played dress-up. The bottom of the trunk is lined with off-white crocheted doilies. Grandma tried to teach me the art of crochet, but she said my fingers were too stubby.

Grandma's prized possession . . . her eyes always misted when she took it out of the trunk . . . was her mother's old family Bible. The cover was tattered; the pages were smudged by countless pressed flowers. (Grandma explained how her mom would always place a flower from one of her loved ones' funeral in the Bible and enter the death on the last page of the Holy Book — the list was long.) I know one day soon I will be placing a yellow rose in this precious book. It seems very important that one of Grandma's favorite flowers joins her ancestral bouquet in the Bible.

I don't know why people have to grow old and die. And I think at least they deserve to spend their last years living in dignity — not suffering from a tragic disease like Alzheimer's. It robs the warmth, the personality, the very life from loving souls. But it can't completely take Grandma away from me because, you see, I have her beloved trunk!

10

DOGS . . . ARE THEY REALLY MAN'S BEST FRIEND?

1 I don't want to be disloyal to our canine friends, but who
2 started the rumor that a guy's best buddy was a dog? Would a
3 *true* friend chew up your socks, bury your unmentionables in
4 the garden and leave his calling card in your front yard?
5 And why don't the mighty cat lovers of America rise up
6 and proclaim Felix and Morris to be man's best companion?
7 They don't chew at the postman's ankle, raise their hind leg on
8 Grandma's antique coffee table, or howl at the moon till the
9 neighbors call the cops. They don't need rhinestone leashes or
10 flea collars. No weekly trips to the groomers to have fancy
11 ribbons put in their hair. There are other creatures out there,
12 too, who might deserve the "best amigo" title . . . what's wrong
13 with a goldfish, monkey or turtle? I think we're talking
14 prejudice and discrimination here. I can see it all now . . .
15 protesting bunnies, parrots and skunks marching down
16 Pennsylvania Avenue demanding equal rights!
17 I'm sure this "doggie dilemma" got its start when Lassie
18 came home and Rin Tin Tin jumped in on all fours and made
19 a courageous rescue. (But remember, Mighty Mouse was always
20 there to save the day, too!) And now we have Beethoven's antics
21 and Hooch slobbering all over the screen.
22 Music played its part in this puppy popularity thing. There
23 was never a song about a parakeet that could bring tears to
24 my eyes like my granddad singing "Old Shep." (In all fairness,
25 it might have been Granddad's singing instead of the sad lyrics.)
26 And, of course, "How Much Is That Gator in the Window?"
27 never would have made it to the top of the charts. But the
28 clincher, the song that made Elvis and Alpo eaters everywhere
29 forever famous, that made all other living creatures losers in
30 the pet parade — "You Ain't Nothing but a Hound Dog"!
31 I'd like to tell all you little feathery critters, you four-legged
32 felines, you underwater fin fellows and all other would-be pets

1 **. . . you don't have a chance! Dogs will always dominate. They**
2 **have since the first fire hydrant. So put down your protest**
3 **posters and just accept being runner-up . . . and maybe**
4 **someday the human population will wise up and let you have**
5 **your moment in the sun. Remember, every dog has his day!**
6
7
8
9
10
11
12
13
14
15
16
17
18
19
20
21
22
23
24
25
26
27
28
29
30
31
32
33
34
35

11

OH, FOR THE '50S AGAIN!

1 I just love to hear my aunts talk about the "good old
2 days" — the '50s! To hear them tell it, life was a lot simpler for
3 teenagers back then — no AIDS or drugs; just had to worry
4 about having enough starched petticoats to hold your poodle
5 skirt away from your bobby-soxed legs. They hadn't invented
6 pantyhose yet, but they did have those dreadful garter belts — I
7 saw one in the Smithsonian and at Frederick's!
8 School had to be a lot less complicated . . . just pushing
9 the old three Rs — no computers and technology to clog up a
10 girl's brainwaves. You see, females weren't expected to take
11 any courses but shorthand and bookkeeping in the "Beaver
12 Cleaver" days. I know it was a chauvinistic attitude, but it sure
13 would have taken the academic pressure off! That old "Be all
14 you can be" was strictly for the male gender; the weaker sex
15 didn't have to prove a thing — after all, they were only girls!
16 Other things were different, too. For instance, hair styles!
17 No long hours of crimping and conditioning; just a bouncy
18 ponytail behind a turned-up collar. And the music — no hard
19 rock or mind-boggling X-rated raps; just simple tunes like "It
20 Takes Two to Tango," "Mule Train" and "Smoke Gets in Your
21 Eyes." Heroes were different — there were no Michael Jordans
22 and Magic Johnsons. Kids looked up to Roy Rogers, Gene
23 Autrey and Elvis.
24 And teenagers read . . . OK, so sometimes it was just comic
25 books. Everybody on the block had a collection of *Superman*
26 and *Archie* comics. (My aunts saved theirs, and they are worth
27 big bucks today!) Television was just getting its start, so what
28 else was a kid to do but read? But when TV hit, it caused quite
29 a sensation. I guess the whole family used to come whether
30 invited or not on Saturday night to Aunt Susan's to watch
31 *Lawrence Welk*. It was a big change from gathering around
32 the radio to listen to *Amos and Andy* or *Our Miss Brooks*.
33 Dating was different in the '50s, too. For one thing, girls

1 **had no choice but to sit by the phone and wait for Mr. Right**
2 **(or Mr. Wrong) to call. My aunts said they wore the cushioned**
3 **seat out of three chairs during their dating years. Grandma**
4 **always told them signs of aggressiveness on a girl's part made**
5 **her look cheap! (Having pierced ears, Grandma also said, was**
6 **a one-way ticket to hell.) Both aunts waited until after their**
7 **fiftieth birthday to have their ears pierced — after Grandma**
8 **went to the big clip-on place in the sky.**
9 **The movies have changed more than anything else, Aunt**
10 **Frances says. She said she and Aunt Susan would go to the big**
11 **musical movies and sing the songs for the next week, and all**
12 **teenage girls wanted to be sweet and pure like Doris Day**
13 **instead of hookers and Playboy bunnies! A girl didn't have to**
14 **be embarrassed by the foul language and revealing bedroom**
15 **scenes when sitting by a date. Aunt Susan said if the scene**
16 **started to fade or a waterfall sprang up, you knew something**
17 **was happening — probably involving S-E-X — but you weren't**
18 **exactly sure what!**
19 **So, all things considered, I think I would truly have**
20 **enjoyed being a teenager during this magical era. But since I'm**
21 **a '90s kind of girl, I'll just have to make do and try to organize**
22 **a '50s day every year at our school!**
23
24
25
26
27
28
29
30
31
32
33
34
35

12

GREAT EXPECTATIONS

I've got to get away from this place. I know it's my home and if I run away my mother will have a nervous breakdown, but if I stay I will explode . . . self-destruct! I can't live with my father any longer. He's too demanding; I can never please him no matter how hard I try. Mom says it's not all his fault — he's a perfectionist and expects the same of others . . . especially his sons. But I say it *is* his fault for being so stubborn and being so certain that he's *always* right! Luckily, Brad was able to live up to all of his high goals and ideals . . . but *I'm not Brad*! I've tried to explain this to him, but as usual he turns a deaf ear to anything I say.

All of our lives our family has had to cater to Dad's only-one-way, my-way attitude and his quick temper. I wish I could just shrug him off when he's mad like Mom and Brad do, but I can't. I think normal people should be able to control their tempers . . . or at least not take their anger out on their family. If anything goes wrong, from a B in algebra to a flat tire, Dad's on the rampage and the whole family has to tiptoe around until he settles down! And needless to say, my whole existence has caused major flare-ups!

I'm really sorry I've been such a big disappointment to the head of our house. I would have liked to be like Brad, but I couldn't play baseball as well, run as fast or keep my room as neat. I had no interest in Boy Scouts, FFA or the debate team — all a direct route to my dad's heart! My skills in auto mechanics, poetry writing and being a stand-up comic were wasted on someone as single-minded as my father. My dad has a rigid idea of right and wrong — his way is right . . . anything else is out of the question. My mom has a record she plays all the time by some old-time singer like Frank Sinatra titled "My Way" . . . I think it should be Dad's theme song.

Don't get me wrong, I love my dad . . . I just don't always like him. I just wish he could accept me for what I am . . .

everybody else thinks I'm a funny, creative guy. I have lots of friends — I wish Dad was one of them. I guess I'll try a little harder, give our relationship one last chance. I know deep down Dad wants what's best for me; he's just sure he's the only one who knows what that happens to be!

Father's Day is coming up soon; maybe I'll write him a poem . . . try to explain how I feel. He's in the den now; maybe if I went in and tried to talk to him . . . if just once he'd listen. I'll give it a shot . . . for Mom's sake, for my sake, for Dad's sake. "Dad, Dad, do you have a minute? We need to talk."

13

GUYS ARE SCUM

1 I've had it with the males of the world — they are all
2 jerks . . . low lifes . . . demented banana brains! I'm through
3 nurturing their macho attitudes and pretending to be interested
4 in their two-syllable-word conversations. I'm tired of looking
5 up at inflated egos. I'm sick to death of holding back my
6 personality to make room for their over-emphasized self-image.
7 It's over . . . I'm going to forget guys ever existed. I'll think of
8 them as magnificent creatures who roamed the earth, but were
9 so lacking in intellectual skills they became extinct . . . much
10 like the dinosaur.
11 I could (and maybe I will) write a sensational best seller
12 of all the dirty tricks guys have played on me and others of the
13 female species. Kyle took Natalie to the drive-in . . . in Cindy's
14 car. Jose gave the love poem he wrote for Margarite to six other
15 girls in different schools. Steven was going steady with three
16 girls at the same time. (I was one of them!) He got by with it till
17 he got his schedules mixed! (Remember about the dinosaurs?)
18 Khan dated Marti when he was flunking geometry, Pam when
19 his English grade was in jeopardy and "fast" Frannie when he
20 needed help with his sex ed project! And the stories of
21 deception, infidelity and disloyalty go on and on and on . . .
22 And I don't have the time to get into a discussion about
23 the male taste in music and movies . . . their life-long love affairs
24 with cars . . . their addictions to sports.
25 I know, I know . . . somewhere out there one might find a
26 few guys who could measure higher than a zero on the ten-point
27 "male scale." My own father, for instance, on a good day, could
28 pull a four. My brother, on the other hand, rates a minus three.
29 I suppose if a girl went on a nationwide quest with a "guy-go-
30 counter," looking for high-scoring males, she'd find a few. But
31 my guess is they'd be stuffed and on display in museums or
32 earmarked for the priesthood!
33 I would like to think that there's hope for *man*kind . . . but

I've seen little evidence to sustain that hope. Guys are still out there lying, bragging, two-timing . . . and, of course, like in Grandma's day, they still only want *one* thing from a girl — *undying adoration*! Like rats need cheese . . . like Superman needs a phone booth . . . like Dolly Parton needs support . . . guys need praise and compliments. I think it has something to do with that missing rib . . . if it hadn't bit the dust, so to speak, perhaps things would be different. Maybe guys would be different; maybe we could learn to depend on them . . . count on them to do what they say they'll do . . . actually trust them with our lives, our money and our best friend! But, they *don't* have the rib, and since it was tied to their brain and conscience, those important ingredients went, too. So, until they make a new model, get a new and improved product, we girls will just have to go on strike, or shut up and put up with their fluky flaws.

14

OVERTHROWING THE SCHOOL CAFETERIA

1 The day is going to come when we're going to have to do
2 something about the cafeteria food. We've choked it down since
3 we were old enough to hold a dented fork . . . we've swallowed
4 it long before we understood about "taste buds," and we've
5 chewed and chewed and chewed until we're ready to spit up
6 and spit out the whole concept of "school lunch"! Yes, we've
7 endured it for eleven years — we're talking stringy spinach,
8 lumpy potatoes, and *mystery meat* — and now the time has
9 come to revolt from that revolting substance we call school slop!
10 We've always wondered where they get the stuff they so
11 cheerfully glob on our trays each day. Do they rinse out old
12 milk bottles to make the gravy? Do they raid the garbage barrels
13 behind fast food places at night to get their weekly "surprise"
14 dishes? Do they scrape road kill from the highways to make
15 their indigestible casseroles? And do they recycle Alpo to
16 streeeetch the meatloaf? These and other questions are things
17 inquiring teenage minds want to know.
18 Then, there are the *sightings*! Yes, those wee bits of foreign
19 matter strategically placed among the green beans, mixed in
20 with the creamed corn, sprinkled atop the baked beans. We're
21 talking twilight zone objects here! Karen found some
22 unidentifiable furry thing in her meat patty; Keith found
23 enough hair in his stuffing to make a toupee for his bald
24 grandfather; Sara spotted the fingernail in her broccoli-cheese
25 delight before she bit into it! Then there are the protein
26 additions — cockroaches, flies and the occasional worm!
27 I say we've kept our mouths shut too long . . . except when
28 we were shoveling that "stuff" they call food down our
29 esophagi. We need to band together and change the menus and
30 the recipes . . . or *get* some recipes that taste like real food from
31 our moms, our great-aunts, our grandmothers, our sisters. (No,
32 scratch that idea. My sister's food is even worse than cafeteria
33 food. Her sloppy joes killed our cat and caused Spotty to spend

four days in the doggie hospital!) I know for a fact that my Granny could take over the school kitchen and feed the whole student body the best spaghetti and meatballs, the best chicken-fried steak, the best chocolate cream pie. I've seen her do it at family reunions . . . and we have a *big* family. Yep, she's another one who could feed the masses with a few fishsticks and a handful of bread crumbs!

There would be no more complaints, groans, quick trips to the latrine, tossing of Tums down the gullet or use of barf bags if my grandmother was in charge of our nutritional needs. Everybody would be asking for big helpings and coming back for seconds. They'd still be groaning after lunch . . . but from overeating, not from indigestion or food poisoning!

So let's start a good food campaign . . . make posters, picket, write slogans like "Play Your Hunch — Avoid School Lunch" or "Cafeteria Food Has No Reason or Rhyme — It's Just Made of Sewer Slime."

We *can* win and we owe it to our stomachs to try. And I'll talk to my granny. She's retired . . . doesn't do anything but fly to Vegas for long weekends and play Bingo at the VFW. But until we get some changes made, my best advice to all of you: *Bring a sack lunch*!

15

SWEET DREAMS, PUTT

I guess this is good-bye, Putt. Don't try to get up, boy. The doctor said that shot will work pretty fast. 'Atta boy . . . just lie there and think about all the good times we've had — the rabbit chases, the mountain climbing, the sock chewing. Yep, you were an ornery little cuss when you were a pup. You ate a chair in Dad's den, knocked over all the wastebaskets in the house hourly, chewed up Mom's Legg's Control Tops every time she hung them over the shower rod. And you got half of your daily nutrition from footwear — socks, slippers, galoshes, thongs. You loved them all. Boy, were we glad when your chewing days were over; we were both always in the dog house with Mom!

I'm really going to miss you, Putt. The old golf course won't be the same without your little black tail waving down by the flag. Even when I missed, you always made me feel like Jack Nicklaus. You were always waiting up for me at night, even when I sneaked in my bedroom window, and you never said a word about me breaking curfew.

Whoever said a dog was man's best friend must have known you'd be coming along — waiting by the fence to hear my car, recognizing the sound of the Bomb's motor two blocks away. I think I'll be losing one of the best parts of my childhood today, Putt, my best friend. You shared all my secrets, fella, and you were some kind of listener. And you know, after I told you my troubles and looked into your caring eyes, I always felt better. Remember the time I was going to run away from home? I was all packed, then you jumped on my duffle bag and looked up at me with those big, sad eyes. I could have sworn I saw tears. Putt, you were always there for me when I needed you. That's why I insisted on bringing you out here today. We've taken many rides together, boy, but this was a tough one.

Now don't worry. I'll take good care of your dog house, and I'll make sure your favorite bush is watered! I'll retire your favorite leash and doggie dish, and your red ball goes with

you . . . I couldn't stand to see another dog use your stuff.

And Putt, Grandma always said a dog who's loved on earth has a special place in heaven, so you've got no worries there, boy. Your wings are waiting. No dog has been more loved than you, Putt. You're going to leave a big empty space . . . missed by the whole family, everyone on the block, the golf team and every female dog in a nine-block radius. You were an active little bugger. In fact, I've been promised a puppy from Poopsie's litter. You remember the cute little cocker spaniel with the long lashes and swinging hips? Is that a grin, Putt? You do remember Poopsie, you devil, you!

I don't know about the pup. Nobody's going to be able to take your place, Putt. You're grinning again . . . you think the puppy's a good idea? Well, we'll see . . .

Now, here comes the doc, Putt. You take it easy. I'll never forget you. You were the best. Someday I'll tell my son all about you. Now, you have a good rest, Putt . . . sweet dreams . . .

16

SURE-FIRE EXCUSES FOR NOT HAVING YOUR HOMEWORK DONE

1 How many of you have been in trouble for not having your
2 homework done? I knew it . . . it's a universal problem. And it's
3 always worse if you don't have a ready excuse — one that will
4 make the teacher not only believe you, but want to give you
5 either extra time or, better yet, *extra credit*!
6 Now, you can throw out the old stand-bys that your
7 grandfather used — "I lost it," or "The dog ate it." They are as
8 obsolete as dunce caps. You're going to have to update your
9 act if you want to be a success as a homework dodger. Excuses
10 often depend on gender. Girls can get by with the occasional,
11 "I left it in my other notebook." Guys never have even *one*
12 notebook and teachers know this, so members of the male sex
13 have to be a little more creative. And as luck would have it,
14 they're the ones who are most in need of good excuses!
15 On a rare occasion the old health routine works — "I had
16 a migraine last night," or "I got ptomaine poisoning at the local
17 Taco Shell." Then, too, a relative's illness, emergency or demise
18 will work *once* (but only once). These teachers keep track of
19 how many grandmas you have, and they do check the obituary
20 columns.
21 The old "My mother ran it through the Maytag" is wearing
22 a little thin, but it might work on a first-year teacher. The "I
23 dribbled root beer, spaghetti sauce or tapioca pudding all over
24 it" is a pretty sticky excuse, too. Sometimes a new baby brother
25 or puppy upchucking on it is good for one missing assignment
26 (be sure to bring a picture of the newborn).
27 Some kids just have the magic touch when it comes to
28 far-out excuses. Margaret got by with "I was held at gun point,
29 and they took my purse, the ring my great grandmother gave
30 me and my geometry assignment!" Carl slipped through with
31 "A homeless person needed some sturdy paper for the holes in
32 his shoes . . . and being the humanitarian I am, I fished out and

sacrificed my finished English theme!" But my all-time favorite is Freddy's "We ran out of Charmin . . . and please, please don't punish me any more, Miss Bates. I've suffered enough . . . I have paper cuts!"

So if you'll stretch your imagination, free your creative soul, you, too, can come up with a good excuse and get by without doing your homework. Good luck. I've got to go — my unfinished math paper is in the neighbor's rabbit cage . . . I'm hoping it will multiply!

17

GIRLS GET ALL THE HALOES

1 It's not fair . . . girls have it made. They can be good
2 without even trying. We gave them our *good* rib, and God gave
3 them wings, and us guys got the whiskers! They can spit polish
4 their gift once a year, but we he-men have to mow these manly
5 beards every morning.
6 And girls just look innocent. It's all that blush they put
7 on — gives their faces a wholesome, "cherubic" look. Guys'
8 mugs are usually nicked by our Bics! They don't have to wrestle,
9 lift weights or play football to prove their manhood. Knitting
10 and gossiping on the phone doesn't call for a very tough
11 exterior. They don't have to fight to prove they're macho. To
12 avoid whimpdom they just flap their lips or sharpen their razor-
13 edged tongues. Girls are mostly mouth when it comes to any
14 sort of confrontation. But we Rocky look-alikes have to flex
15 and fight! We can't get by sitting on dainty, little cushions
16 tossing chocolate-covered cherries down our throats while the
17 soaps are on.
18 Teachers automatically favor girls. How many of them do
19 you see lined up in the principal's office? How many are forced
20 to stay after school and dust erasers or dig old gum from under
21 the desks? Girls can get away with whispering, note-passing
22 and coming in late. And they can always get a hall pass. If a
23 guy asks for one, the teachers assume he wants free time to
24 paint the principal's graven image above the urinals or to stop
25 up the school sewer with bubble gum!
26 Parents are just as bad. When they see the blue blanket
27 in the hospital nursery, it's like they make a pact to not cut
28 that manchild any slack. But when "baby pink blanket" arrives,
29 shower the little princess with trust, praise and Grandma's
30 diamond brooch!
31 It's no use . . . since Eve dished up the applesauce, guys
32 have had to prove themselves while the female gender needs
33 only to bat their eyes, give one of those me-do-anything-wrong?

looks they've spent hours practicing before their mirrors. Girls are innocent even when they're proven guilty. Guys are sentenced without a hearing! The sugar and spice vs. snails and puppy-dog tails verse was one the world sure bit into. And that old "boys will be boys . . . so let's nail them" routine can be witnessed every day.

So you see, the girls get the glory, the guys get the shaft. The females win the good conduct medals and awards; we fellows are spectators. It truly is a woman's world. They've taken over. We're only little puffs of "wind beneath their wings"!

But it's OK, guys. It's our own fault, really. We let it happen. We could try harder . . . care enough to be our very best! We could be the ones kissing up to teachers and parents. We could be on the Dean's List, Who's Who, win citizenship awards. But frankly, we're better off playing second fiddle . . . less stress. Let the women rule the universe. Let's go bowling, grab a pizza, see the Bears game. The pressure's off. Let the gals have the headaches, conquer the dragons. We really lucked out, guys!

18

SUBSTITUTE MOTHERS

I know why they're called "step" mothers . . . because they walk all over you! Yes, these *new* women that hypnotize and trap weak men like my father should be locked up. They're really dangerous . . . they should come with a surgeon general's warning label. I know if Teresa had not come along with her little flirty bag of tricks my dad would have come to his senses and gone begging on his knees for Mom to give him another chance. Of course, Mom swore she wouldn't take him back under any circumstances, but I think she just said that to protect her pride. It's too late now, anyway . . . Dad went to Las Vegas two months ago and married the other woman! And now my life has changed forever: victim of a broken home . . . weekend father . . . and like Cinderella I now have a *stepmother*!

Now she's always there when I go visit Dad on weekends . . . hanging all over him and calling him mushy, little stupid names like "huggems"! It makes me gag, but Dad's so dense he eats it up like a starved cat turned loose in a dairy barn. Then there's that kid — Abbey! She's only six, and if Teresa's not on Dad's lap, Abbey is, and she calls him Daddy! He doesn't have any time for me now. I'm just that other girl he sends a monthly child support check to. Teresa will probably try to get those stopped because she's a spendaholic! You should see her wardrobe! She took Abbey and me shopping last Saturday, and she really kept Dad's Visa card hot! I will have to admit that she was very generous with my father's money! I got three new outfits right down to the shoes. Mom was mad; she said, "Your dad would have cut up the credit cards if I'd gone on a spending spree like that!" Mom and her other divorced friends are always talking about how easy the second wife has it. They all read a book — *First Wives' Club* — and entered the contest the author had about how badly the first wife was treated. I saw the winners on a talk show. Actually, Dad didn't treat Mom all that

bad, but I don't dare tell her that!

I guess I'll have to learn to get along with Teresa. I don't want to lose Daddy, and I think she's there to stay. (Of course, I thought Mom was, too!) And I guess she's not that bad. She can't cook . . . it's funny to see Dad in the kitchen making Mom's potato salad for another woman — strange world!

And I must admit it's kind of nice to have a little runt like Abbey looking up to me. I braided her hair last week and polished her nails Melt-Your-Heart Pink. Now, she's my slave for life. So, I guess I'll have to dig out a couple of my old dolls. I'll have to sneak them out of the house; Mom'd flip if she saw me taking supplies to the enemy camp!

I still wish Dad was here and we were a "normal" family, but I guess divorce is just a fact of life now with my folks' generation. I hope kids my age can turn that around — sure would save lots of heartache for kids like me. Well, I'd better get my bag packed. It's time to go to my "other" mother's house. I hope she doesn't try to cook! Maybe she'll let me experiment with her makeup. I guess it's not *so* bad having two moms!

19

THIS LITTLE PIGGY

1 A funny thought occurred to me at Grandma's dining room
2 table last night. When she brought the chicken platter and
3 everybody was forking his favorite chicken part, it reminded
4 me that I also have my favorite girl parts — the feet! I know, I
5 know, most of you are "leg men" or upper body torso admirers,
6 and a few of you are suckers for long, flowing hair or oval eyes
7 with lashes as thick as broom straws. But to me nothing is as
8 exciting as cute, little chubby toes lacquered with candy-apple
9 nail polish.
10 I'm probably in the minority, but somewhere there must
11 be others who are "turned on" by the sight of little up-turned
12 toes peeking out of open-toed sandals. I'm sure I'm the only
13 guy in the midwest who has the guts to admit: *I like girls' feet!*
14 Wait, let me clarify that. I don't like *all* types of female hooves.
15 For instance, I hate long, skinny feet with toes like a witch's
16 fingers. You've seen them . . . ones that look like AmTrak gave
17 them the once over. My Aunt Floy has a couple of feet like that,
18 and she says they are very time saving . . . she picks up
19 scattered socks, flushes the toilet and waves "bye-bye" with
20 her finger-like toes! Feet like these may be useful, but they are
21 super ugly. If Henry the Eighth's wives would have had feet
22 like these, he'd have had them befooted! If Eve's feet had looked
23 like hands, Adam would have shared someone else's Jonathan!
24 Now, let's get back to the *good* feet. I'm sure Juliet had
25 small, dainty tootsies. And you'd never see Wonder Woman or
26 Tarzan's Jane swingin' on ropes with their long toes flappin'
27 in the breeze.
28 I'm sure by now you all think I need therapy . . . don't
29 suggest it to my mom! I hope I've given you some food for
30 thought, and I want to add this one last "foot note." If you think
31 I'm the only guy who feels this way, you're wrong. Turn on
32 your TV sometime and look for my fellow foot fancier, Al
33 Bundy!

20

I DON'T WANT TO INHERIT MOM'S CELLULITE!

1 Oh, no. I've gained another pound! Look at this leg. I'm
2 beginning to grow cellulite like a Kansas farmer grows wheat.
3 They'll be calling me Cottage Cheese Legs in gym. My fanny
4 will start jiggling when I walk like Sara's. It was probably that
5 Snickers bar . . . or maybe the last three Snickers bars! I do
6 love those suckers when they're frozen like a
7 popsicle . . . ummm, gotta quit thinking about them. Sure, I've
8 been counting my fat grams . . . of course, math is my worst
9 class! I love home ec . . . especially the cooking and the eating!
10 There I go again. I'm a glutton . . . completely obsessed with
11 the idea of food.
12 It's really Mom's fault. She didn't even try to keep me a
13 trim baby. She said she loved fat-cheeked, dimple-thighed wee
14 ones. My baby pictures look like little chipmunks with the
15 mumps! Then there are those X-rated shots: my chubby little
16 bun cheeks exposed on a bear-skin rug . . . Mom's favorites to
17 drag out when company arrives! Someday those pictures will
18 mysteriously disappear from the family album. I'll replace them
19 with ones I secretly took of Mom trying on swimsuits! Revenge
20 is the only sweet taste that doesn't put on pounds!
21 Another problem: Mom and Grandma are excellent cooks.
22 Mom makes a lasagne to die for, and Gram's coconut cream
23 pies are legendary. How can a girl keep trim when gourmet
24 food is being passed under her nose?
25 I do work out now, and Mom bought all those aerobics
26 tapes . . . something we could do together . . . a little mother/
27 daughter project! But it wasn't a success. Mom always fixed us
28 hot fudge sundaes afterwards. She said we worked hard and
29 deserved a reward! So, you see, I've got to do something about
30 my mother or I'll be doing all of my shopping at the Lots to
31 Love shop. Don't get me wrong. I love my mother . . . she's a
32 peach . . . peach cobbler is another of her claims to fame! But

1 I don't want hips decorated with little fat globs.
2 So I'm going to have to sit Mom down and have a heart-to-
3 heart . . . like when we had our "You're turning into a woman"
4 talk. I'll simply say, "Mom, let's cut out the chips, ice cream
5 and cookies when we buy groceries. Instead, let's load the
6 shopping cart with yogurt, veggies and fruit. You'll be doing
7 Dad a big favor, too. He needs to watch out for his heart . . . yes,
8 I *know* you have that big life insurance policy on him! But get
9 serious, Mom, you and Dad can go back to eating cholesterol
10 when I go to college next year. It'll give you something to look
11 forward to in your old age!" Yep, I'll go right into the kitchen
12 now while I have my courage up . . . tell her to take off her Betty
13 Crocker costume and become a Jane Fonda mother. Maybe
14 it'd help if we went to the mall and tried on leotards! One look
15 at her buns in a three-way mirror and Mom'd have to start a
16 serious, fat-free diet. The shock might be too much for her
17 heart, but Dad does have that insurance policy!
18 Well, here goes . . . a girl's gotta do what a girl's gotta do.
19 "Mom, Mom, do you have time for a little 'girl talk'?" What's
20 that she's baking? Oh, no, I'm sunk. It's double-decker
21 chocolate fudge brownies! "Sure, I want to lick the bowl.
22 Where's the spoon? Oh, it was nothing, Mom. We can talk
23 tomorrow."
24
25
26
27
28
29
30
31
32
33
34
35

21

IT'S HARD TO SAY GOOD-BYE

1 God, please . . . don't make me do this. I know Tammy and
2 I took an oath at the age of eight to always be there for each
3 other. And I've never failed her . . . until now. I've been to her
4 birthday parties since we were seven years old. I went to all
5 those slumber parties she gave in her cold, unfinished
6 basement. I was there when she chipped her front tooth on a
7 swing in the park. I stood beside her when we had our smallpox
8 shots. I held her hand through *Halloween I* and *II* and gave
9 her my towel in P.E. when hers fell in the toilet.
10 I cried with her when her Granny had a heart attack and
11 never came out of a coma. I split my weekly pack of M & Ms,
12 and she always got the first sip of my Pepsi. And when Tammy
13 said, "Want to hear a secret?," I never told it to anybody but
14 my diary. Believe me, God, there isn't anything I wouldn't do
15 for my best friend, Tammy . . . except . . . except . . . attend her
16 funeral.
17 Maybe if I shut my eyes real tight I'll wake up and find it
18 was all some horrible dream. Maybe this time Tammy will
19 refuse to ride home from the party with Fred. I blame myself,
20 God. I told her Fred had been drinking . . . that she should ride
21 with me. But I should have tried harder. I should have forced
22 her into my car. But she was so flattered that a stud football
23 player was paying attention to her and thrilled when he asked
24 to take her home. Tammy's diary was stuffed with pages about
25 her crush on Fred. He'd been the guy of her dreams since junior
26 high — well, he and Rhett Butler. (Tammy and I watched *Gone*
27 *With the Wind* seven times the summer between seventh and
28 eighth grades.)
29 She *knew* all about the dangers of driving and drinking.
30 We've attended every "just say no" meeting. Tammy never was
31 one to give in to peer pressure . . . why, she was a leader in
32 S.A.D.D.
33 God, why? Why would you take somebody like Tammy?

She was just getting started in life . . . and she loved everybody. Mom says only the good die young, but it's just not fair. She was just taking her first classes toward her law degree. She'd worked so hard to lose twenty pounds. She looked so pretty that night at the party. But . . . but . . . she looked so pale . . . so wax-like . . . so silent . . . in that tiny box.

I can't believe that I'll never dial 227-2296 again . . . that I'll never hear her horn tooting to pick me up in the morning. Who's going to help me solve my dating problems? Who'll be there with a funny story to make the hurt go away when I get dumped or flunk a chemistry test? Who's going to share tomorrow's dreams and yesterday's disappointments?

Well, I guess it's time . . . to say my final farewell to the best friend a girl ever had. We won't be wearing those goofy matching T-shirts to the senior barbecue. There'll be no cheery face in the next row smiling through tears at the graduation ceremony . . . nobody to stand beside me in cap and gown for friendship pictures . . .

We'll never be roommates at college now — sorority sisters — but that doesn't really matter because we've been more than sisters all these years, Tammy. We've shared our sack lunches, our clothes, our homework and most of all, our dreams. How many hours have we spent on the phone . . . cheering each other up when we'd had a bad day, congratulating each other when someone special happened to speak to us in the hall. I don't want it to be over; I'm not ready to give you up, Tammy! It's going to be so hard. I don't know what I can do for you now, Tammy . . . the flowers weren't enough. Maybe . . . maybe the only way to do something for you now is to try to fulfill both our dreams. I'll try not to let you down . . . and Tammy, please, save a place for me, so someday we can be roommates in heaven.

22

SINKING SUBS

Substitute teachers are an easy target for teenagers with devious minds . . . and all teenagers have devious minds so subs *beware*!

The news spreads fast whenever a sub is spotted in the hallway. The spotting is the easy part: lost look, fear in the eyes, Substitute Kit grasped tightly in their white knuckles. This kit consists of seasick pills, extra writing assignments, smelling salts, tranquilizers and pain killers. What they *really* need is handcuffs, a bull whip and a 357 Magnum! They come in looking so hopeful, but at three-thirty those who last the day look like someone who got a couple of whiffs of the gas chamber . . . and begged for more!

When a sub is sighted, the speculation begins: Who's gone? Do they just have the sniffles or are we talking embalming fluid? Could we be lucky enough to have it be the calculus teacher or the senior English know-it-all-and-forcing-it-down-our-throats instructor? Or what's really fun is to have one in foreign language. They can never speak it . . . we can't either, so it's party time! Having one in P.E. is good for a dodge-ball-free-for-all. And driver's ed subs give new meaning to highway hysteria!

I don't know *why* anyone would choose to become a substitute. Are they just lost souls with a death wish? Real teachers who couldn't pass the chalkdust test? Or just Evil Kneivel daredevils looking for the ultimate challenge? Whatever their sad tale, we teenagers look on it as our duty to God and country to sabotage, humiliate and disorient whenever possible.

There are classic legends of "sub sinking" in every school. Orchestrated book dropping, seating-chart switching, pencil breaking, gum chewing and spit-wad throwing are standard procedure in "sub" territory. But it's best to go beyond ordinary actions . . . we give merit badges for outstanding achievement. Tony got last year's coveted "Torpedo" for filling Ms. Riley's

1 grade-book drawer with frogs. That substitute has never
2 returned . . . word has it she croaked! Frank loves the whoopie
3 cushion routine. It doesn't win any prizes, but it's always good
4 for a laugh. Todd hid an alarm clock in Mr. Young's bottom
5 desk drawer. It went off in the middle of the hour . . . the sub
6 never did find it! But the class sure chimed in with helpful hints
7 and remarks! What fun! Then the old "kick me" signs on the
8 back have become new and improved — "Pity me, I'm
9 SUBhuman!" "Subs are sandwiches waiting for mayo!"
10 On a rare occasion subs have withstood all of our schemes
11 of torture and actually returned the next day. We admire this
12 kind of dedication . . . these rare birds returning for the encore
13 treatment are either brain dead or hungry! The second day
14 usually convinces them that it wasn't some Edgar Allan Poe
15 nightmare, and they get a job at Wal-Mart! But I must give the
16 devil his due; one sub did best us. We were in top form . . . it
17 was last period of a looong day . . . tonsils were straining . . .
18 mass cheating . . . paper airplanes filled the sky. In other words,
19 it was your regular last-hour-Friday-with-a-sub-in-charge day!
20 But in the middle of the pandemonium, Mr. Keels leaps on the
21 teacher's desk and lets out a Tarzan yell. We froze in our
22 delinquent tracks. We thought he'd finally flipped. But to our
23 amazement, he said in a stern voice, "If we have absolute silence
24 and order in this class till bell time, I will give everyone a
25 five-dollar bill as he/she leaves." This got our attention. Our
26 greedy little hearts started pounding and our obnoxious little
27 mouths sealed like a piece of Tupperware after it's burped. I
28 mean, nobody whispered or spoke or even sneezed. It was the
29 longest and quietest twenty-five minutes on record in our
30 school, but visions of dollar signs danced in our miserly minds.
31 At last the bell rang, and before we could get our money-
32 grubbing fingers out to receive our just desserts, Mr. Keel again
33 jumped on the desk, looked into our anxious, money-hungry
34 eyes and said softly, "I lied!"
35 I don't know whatever happened to Mr. Keels, but that

day he won our respect. Somebody said he went into politics. But we'll always remember the one sub we couldn't sink!

23

WHAT'S WRONG WITH TEENAGE GIRLS?

Don't get me wrong, I *like* teenage girls. They've got a lot of things going for them: shapely bodies, soft voices, sexy eyelashes . . . and they smell good! But if I could make only a *few* changes . . . Don't get upset, ladies, I'm not talking plastic surgery or extensive therapy . . . just a snip, snip here and a snip, snip there in your personalities, conduct, ways you think and act — nothing drastic!

For instance, the giggling. Whenever more than two girls join forces, everything's funny! They snicker at everything, and a fellow always thinks they're laughing at him. (And, in my case, according to my sister, they are!) They giggle in class, they giggle in church . . . at school dances, at ballgames . . . and I've never observed them at funerals, but I wouldn't be one bit surprised! So I think I have a legitimate complaint. If they could just learn to hold the laughter down to a smile or a short lady-like laugh, we fellows would sure appreciate it!

And *gossip*. Whenever my sister gets together with her friends, it's one big back-stabbing party. (Caesar could have been their guest of honor!) Anybody who isn't present is "fair game." They're all afraid to go to the "little girl's room" for fear of having their most intimate secrets revealed and later printed in the "Snoop's Corner" of the school paper. I don't know how it happens, but whenever teenage girls (or even antique girls like my mom) congregate en masse they turn into reputation-wrecking womenfolk! It must be the Wicked Tongue Fairy working overtime! It's really bad when they have slumber parties — a strange name for an all-night chit-chat session! I once hid my camcorder at one of my sister's all-nighters. I had enough blackmail material to last me till my retirement years, but unfortunately my mom caught me doing my Spielberg bit and, needless to say, my filming days are over!

Also, teenage girls tick us guys off with their we're-too-good-to-be-breathing-the-same-air-as-you-low-life attitude. It's

1 true the football quarterbacks, basketball captains and a few
2 other campus studs don't see this Miss America complex (most
3 females are closet snobs), but mere mortal guys like myself
4 always get looked down on from on high by the self-appointed
5 Celestial Girls! So we'd really appreciate it if you girls could
6 get your noses out of the clouds and not treat us ordinary
7 fellows like last week's garbage. (You see, it's possible when
8 we come to our ten-year reunion some of you "star sisters"
9 might actually be married to some of us subhuman males! Chew
10 on that, girls!)
11 There are lots of other little traits that could use work:
12 female hairstyles, the way they dress, their "in" with all the
13 teachers, their uncoordination behind the driver's wheel, and
14 the list goes on and on and on. But we are willing to overlook
15 a few flaws!
16 So what do you say, girls? Can you at least *try* to
17 change . . . soften up a little? The teenage guys of America
18 deserve a break today — so lighten up on us. Who knows, if
19 this works, we fellows might even be willing to make a couple
20 of changes . . . well, maybe!
21
22
23
24
25
26
27
28
29
30
31
32
33
34
35

24

DARCI ALWAYS GOT BETTER VALENTINES

Most of us remember someone in our lives who was our biggest rival — our arch enemy. Batman had the Joker, Popeye had Bluto, Archie had Reggie, and I had Darci.

From the second grade on, Darci beat me at everything. It's not that I wasn't successful. I achieved a lot. But Darci was always out in front . . . stealing the gold, leaving me with the silver. If I got to sing a duet, Darci went solo . . . when I was wearing training bras, Darci wore the "real thing" . . . by the time I had my first date, Darci was going steady.

Don't get me wrong, I didn't hate Darci. True, she wasn't my best friend, but we attended the same slumber parties, sat at the same lunch table, and were locker partners in gym. So, you ask, did Darci know she was such a fly in my teenage ointment . . . such an Olympic hurdle that kept tripping my adolescent ego? Of course, she did. She never put it in words, but the smirks when she looked *back* at me, all the you-gave-it-your-best-shot remarks, the "thrill of victory" looks! She knew . . . and she loved it!

Now, am I going to let the teenage rivalry ruin my life? Put me on a psychiatrist's couch? Keep me from coming to class reunions? No, I've come to terms with my second-place status, and I feel good about myself. I can now look at myself in the mirror and see a winner . . . not a runner-up. And I can truthfully say I'm glad Darci came in first all of those times. I'm glad she has a room full of trophies and awards. I'm glad she has memories of successes and accomplishments. You see, Darci will need all of that strength and talent that she has . . . for Darci found out in her junior year she has M.S. She finished out the year in a wheelchair. It was tough going, and a lesser person — someone who wasn't used to fighting to cross the finish line — would have given up. But not Darci. It was one of her greatest victories!

25

I'LL KNOW WHEN I'M MATURE

1 "Grow up, grow up." I'm so tired of having my mom and
2 dad say that! "You'll get more privileges when you act more
3 mature," Dad says when he grounds me for some little nothing
4 I did. Grandma's my best ally when this happens. I just call
5 her and she'll tell me things Dad did that were twice as bad as
6 my "immature" antics! When I refresh Dad's mind about his
7 own colorful youth, it often cuts down my sentence!
8 This whole growing up thing is very confusing to me. One
9 day my folks are telling me to quit acting goofy — be a "man."
10 Then the next day when Dad is working on his income taxes
11 or paying bills he'll say, "Son, don't be in such a big hurry to
12 grow up. Stay a kid as long as you can!"
13 Of course, Dad says my immaturity is a direct result of
14 Mom's babying me. He says she won't let me grow up . . . that
15 she wants to keep me as her "wittle" boy forever! She does tuck
16 me in at night and remind me to say my prayers. And she does
17 cut my steak, but just so I won't choke on a big bite! And I'm
18 not proud of the fact that my mommy still sews my jammies! I
19 know, it's humiliating for somebody who's starting to shave
20 every day to sleep in nightwear covered with little cowboys
21 and Indians! And my mother would still be telling me bedtime
22 stories if I didn't shoo her out of my room so I could dig my
23 girlie magazines from under my mattress! In spite of all that,
24 Mom insists that she's just being a good mother like Wally and
25 the Beav had.
26 Mom says I act so irresponsible because I run around with
27 weird kids. She's right in one way: my friends and I have gotten
28 into a few jams . . . like when we raided the girls' dressing room
29 while they were outside playing softball! We had a nice Playtex
30 collection waving from the flagpole . . . talk about *old glory*!
31 Unfortunately, Mr. Finch did not see the patriotic humor
32 intended, and in his two-hour lecture he brought up Betsy Ross
33 and the meaning of freedom (which we did not experience for

1 the next three months). So, you could say my friends might be
2 a little strange. For instance, Pee Wee does have some bad
3 habits . . . he can chew broccoli and make it come out his nose.
4 (What else is broccoli good for? We even had a president who
5 didn't like it!) Pee Wee can also turn his eyelids wrong-side out
6 and wave bye-bye with his ears! And then there's Binky . . . he's
7 trained his lab, Rascal, to bite girls' buns. But the dog's getting
8 up there in years, and when Ras goes to chew on all those robed
9 buns in the sky, Binky stands a chance of being normal! My
10 friend, Clint, does obscene paintings with colored toothpaste,
11 and Kurt makes disgusting noises with his braces. But none of
12 this proves that my buddies are keeping me from being a man.
13 I'll be taking off for college in another year (I'm leaving
14 the cowboy P.J.s at home), and I'll show everybody how mature
15 I can be. Granny'll open me a banking account so I won't have
16 to beg for pennies on street corners. I work part-time now for
17 Dad, but he puts the money away for safe keeping — says I'm
18 too immature to handle financial matters. I think it's just his
19 way of taking advantage of slave labor!
20 But I'm really looking forward to the day I become an
21 adult . . . the day someone (namely my dad) stands up and says
22 to all the world, "there goes my son . . . he's a *man*!"
23
24
25
26
27
28
29
30
31
32
33
34
35

26

SECRETS I'LL TAKE TO THE GRAVE

1 You know how they say girls can't keep their mouths shut,
2 how they have to tell everything they know and many things
3 they don't? That's sure not true in my case; I can really keep
4 a secret. You can tell me anything and I won't repeat it. For
5 instance, have you heard me breathe a word about my best
6 friend, Julie, slipping out her bedroom window every night to
7 meet an older guy her folks don't like? And I certainly haven't
8 spilled the beans about Jenn's abortion or Sara's mother's
9 affair. And these lips will never repeat seeing my Sunday school
10 teacher, Ms. Atkins, sipping a beverage at Muddy's that wasn't
11 Diet Coke! I would have been a great prisoner of war —
12 splinters under my fingernails wouldn't get out of me that my
13 sister has birth control pills hidden in a Milk Duds box on the
14 third shelf in her closet. Truth serum wouldn't loosen my tongue
15 enough to tell that I spied a fresh box of condoms in my widowed
16 grandmother's bedside table. I guess my ability to have locked
17 lips is just a talent — a gift. Some people have voices like Mariah
18 Carey; others can ice skate in the Olympics. I can listen to a
19 confidential confession and keep it to myself.
20 Needless to say, I'm a popular person . . . a saint, really.
21 A female who listens to earth-shaking gossip and keeps it a
22 secret. Any normal teenage girl with this much smut inside her
23 brain would have to let it leak out through her waggin' tongue
24 or explode! My advanced listening skills save everyone I know
25 time and money that they would have spent on some psychiatrist's
26 couch. It keeps my friends away from sympathetic bartenders
27 and cuts down visits to the confessional booth!
28 Now I know you're wondering what I'm doing with all of
29 this information . . . how I'm processing this "data of dirt" I've
30 pumped out of my relatives and acquaintances! As I said, my
31 lips are sealed, but my fingers have been busy tap, tap, tapping
32 out all of these juicy bits of gossip people have been spouting
33 in my greedy little ears for years! It's all stored in my computer.

Yes, it's all there, every gory tidbit . . . filed away for future reference.

No, no, I'm not planning multiple blackmail! Although . . . No, I'm a Girl Scout, an usher at church, a candy striper. No, my plan for all this gorgeous gossip has nothing to do with a blackmail plot. I am plotting though . . . plotting the biggest blockbuster novel you'll ever read. Watch out Danielle Steele. You don't stand a chance against all this shady, sordid material I've been collecting. I've got enough hot items to fill ten sizzling novels! This town will come alive with buzzing when the first copies hit the stands — guessing who did what, worrying about their hidden sins being exposed at last! That's "pen power" — mightier than old Excalibur!

I've gotta go now. The school counselor just spilled her guts to me. Gotta get it down on a tape while it's fresh in my mind. Now watch for my name on best seller's lists. You'll know that I wrote my details from true happenings, and you know what they say about truth being stranger than fiction! I will change the names to protect the guilty. Yes, thanks to everybody else's past, my future's going to be secure!

27

DAD'S SICK . . . AGAIN

Wow, my third home run tonight . . . I'm hot! Look at Mom and Granddad . . . they're really excited. Looks like Mom got it on video. I'll be able to show my kids that their old man was some kind of hitter in his day. Of course, when I have kids, I'll *be* at all their games; I won't have to watch the tape. Dad promised he'd be here — swore that nothing could keep him away . . . nothing but a date with a bottle. You see, my dad's an alcoholic. See, I can say it, but Dad can't. He's the one who is sick, but our whole family is paying the price.

I used to hate him and think he could stop if he really wanted to. I thought he was the weakest man alive, but I did my senior research project on the disease of alcoholism. I interviewed recovering alcoholics, I attended A.A. meetings, and I read everything I could find on the subject. I made an A on the paper, and most of all, I now understand my father's disease. It really is a disease . . . often more fatal than cancer. And it's a family disease; I really don't know how Mom's stuck it out with him. She's one tough cookie, and she must really love him to take care of him, make excuses for him, listen to all the broken promises. Dad just won't admit he has a drinking problem . . . says he just drinks a little because of the stress at the office. He pretends he never received those three DUIs.

I've made appointment after appointment for him at AA. Even had the counselor come to the house. Dad slammed out the back door. But denial is a common trait among alcoholics. However, I'm not going to give up. Dad means too much to me. Now that I've worked through the anger, I'll never rest till we get Dad on the wagon. I know it's going to be a big task, but I'm up to it. Oh, I'm up to bat again. I feel another homer coming on. Hope Mom has the camera fired up. Tomorrow, when Dad's feeling better, he'll want to see the tape. He'll be real proud of me.

28

DADDY'S LITTLE GIRL

1 *(Sitting with pen and paper)*
2 Dear Daddy,
3 Who'd have thought I'd have to get stamps, paper and
4 envelopes to communicate with my own father? I should be
5 able to run down the hall or out to your shop and tell you
6 anything I want to say. I *really* miss you, Daddy. Are you *sure*
7 you and Mom can't patch things up? Couldn't you go for
8 counseling or talk to a minister? Remember how the two of you
9 used to hug and kiss? I could hardly pry you apart at the movies.
10 I was always embarrassed when my friends visited because
11 the two of you were always all over each other. Surely all those
12 feelings didn't just evaporate. I hear Mom crying in her
13 bedroom every night. Do you cry, too? I sure do. Why did God
14 invent divorce, or was it God? I think it was the devil.
15 Well, enough whining . . . except to say I can't believe you
16 don't live in the same house with us anymore. I miss tripping
17 on your clothes in the den, having to clean up after your
18 midnight scrambled egg binges, and I even miss your off-key
19 singing in the shower! Now you're off to a new job and not even
20 living in the same state. Hope your new surroundings have
21 helped you forget . . . but don't forget me! John Taylor's taking
22 me to the sophomore dance next week. You remember, he's the
23 one you said looked like a character from a Poe story. He's
24 nice and Mom knows his folks . . . and she was impressed with
25 his A in driver's ed.
26 I'm looking forward to seeing you next weekend. Peppy
27 has missed you. She wouldn't eat for two days, but she's
28 beginning to come around. She'll go ape when you drive
29 in . . . so will I! Mom will be at the office, so it won't be awkward,
30 she said. You know Grandma Abbey blames her for everything.
31 She gives her little digs all the time about her cooking, her job,
32 her parenting skills and even her lingerie (said that's what
33 drove you away). But what can you expect . . . she is *your*

mother!

I made an A on my government test and got a small part in the school play. It's only a few lines, but they're funny ones. You can help me rehearse. I want to be really good. You're the only one who understands my strong desire to be an actress. I'm holding you to that promise to send me to California . . . Mom still wants me to be a nurse! Can you imagine me giving shots? I had to hide my eyes when the vet took Peppy's temperature. It was a gross procedure, Dad.

Oh, guess who asked about you? Yep, Ms. Flirty Lips Filson. She's really been nice to me since she found out about the divorce. Don't get too conceited though . . . she swoops down on any guy who's breathing and available. Now about your social life: be choosy and be careful! You haven't dated in centuries and things are different. The women aren't meek like Mom; they're aggressive and won't take no for an answer. And there is AIDS out there . . . use protection. (I've been waiting a long time to get even for that birds and bees lecture you gave me in fifth grade!)

Well, Dad, it seems like I'm going to spend the rest of my life telling you good-bye. I'll see you soon. Take care. I love you. And remember, no matter how old I get, I'll always be . . .

Daddy's Little Girl

FACE DEFEAT . . . OR CHEAT?

1 OK, I'm flipping this coin — heads, I read the three
2 hundred pages in my American history textbook; tails, I tuck
3 this cheat sheet Tony gave me up my sleeve and use it on the
4 test tomorrow!
5 I've never cheated before. Well, there was that one time
6 in second grade when I copied Tommy Wilson's spelling paper.
7 But I learned my lesson: the dork spelled engine I-N-J-U-N!
8 Maybe I should just be more selective in the I.Q.s of the people
9 I'm copying from! Thank goodness these notes aren't Tony's . . .
10 he's on the "most flunked" list! He pays Sara Harris to write
11 crib notes for him . . . and he's making a profit. You see, his
12 Dad pays him ten dollars for every A paper he brings
13 home . . . and Sara only charges five for the notes! He says it's
14 a pretty sweet deal!
15 I don't know why I'm so worried; everybody cheats! Ron
16 writes all of his notes on his handkerchief and always has the
17 sniffles on test day. He usually leaves the classroom with black
18 smudges on his nostrils, but nobody seems to notice . . . and
19 he's always on the honor roll! Doug writes on the palms of his
20 hands, but I'd be so nervous I'd sweat it off . . . I have to spray
21 my hands with Right Guard before I trust myself to hold a girl's
22 hand at a movie! Jon uses the soles of his shoes for important
23 facts, and Tonya writes key words on her fake fingernails.
24 Smitty thinks he's ultra cool — he writes notes on the band of
25 his Fruit of the Looms. None of them ever get caught! Do you
26 think our teachers have eye trouble? Kathy, soloist in our
27 church choir, sticks a cheat sheet in her Bible and asks the
28 teacher if she cares if she reads a little Scripture during the
29 test! So you see, everyone is doing it!
30 So why am I so hesitant? Here's all the important data,
31 neatly typed on this little sheet. And it fits so snugly up the
32 sleeve of my sweater! Such easy access! I'd never get caught.
33 Is it my conscience? Is Jiminy Cricket looking over my

1 **shoulder? Am I afraid my nose will grow another inch? Was it**
2 **the oath I took when I joined the Boy Scouts? Am I afraid my**
3 **grandpa will find out? He is a Baptist minister, you know!**
4 **I've got to stop this right now. I'm as strong as anyone**
5 **else . . . as crafty and coordinated. I can do this — cheat *one***
6 **time, then get on with my life. One little copy session isn't going**
7 **to turn me into a Charles Manson. Of course, I'm not sure how**
8 **he got his start . . . what wrong turn he made.**
9 **Enough of this guilt talk. I'm flipping the coin. It's up to**
10 **you, quarter. Do I study all night or use the cheat sheet? Wait!**
11 **I can't do this . . . I can't flip a coin that has "In God We Trust"**
12 **printed on it. I'm sunk! Mom, bring me some hot chocolate; I've**
13 **got a big test to study for tonight!**
14
15
16
17
18
19
20
21
22
23
24
25
26
27
28
29
30
31
32
33
34
35

30

SOMEDAY I'LL BE THE PERFECT MOM

1 Nobody I know has a perfect Mom. They don't make them
2 like June Cleaver anymore. Many are more like Roseanne.
3 Marci hates her mother because she's a misplaced teenager . . .
4 tries to look as young as Marci, flirts with all her boyfriends
5 and sits in when the girls gather for a gossip session. Cindy's
6 mom is a perfectionist. She makes Cindy keep the house just
7 so-so. She's not allowed to have company because they might
8 leave foot indentations on the carpet! Shanon's mom doesn't
9 care what she does . . . just so Shanon's not under foot when
10 she brings her boyfriends home. Angie's mom is an alcoholic,
11 and Tandy's weighs three hundred pounds and always has
12 them both either gorging on cream puffs and fettucine alfredo
13 or on fat-free diets. Then there's Karen's mother who treats her
14 like a three-year-old, and Molly's mom who makes her raise
15 her three little brothers while the mom partys till dawn.
16 No, moms just aren't made the way they used to be, but
17 I for one intend to be the perfect mother. I'll be caring and yet
18 I'll be fair; I'll be strict enough to give them security, yet flexible
19 enough for life to be fun. I'll be their advisor and their friend;
20 I'll be their caretaker and playmate. I'll set reasonable rules,
21 and most of all I'll *listen* when they talk. I don't want my
22 children to be afraid to come to me with their problems . . . and
23 I'll want them to know that no matter what, I'll always love
24 them.
25 So, I know I'll be a good mother. I'll win Mother of the Year
26 awards . . . I'll pose for Mother's Day posters . . . Hallmark will
27 be writing about me in verse. Yes, I can't wait to be a mother,
28 and when I am, I promise to *be there* for my kids! I promise
29 not to *die* and leave my daughter motherless when she's twelve.
30 I don't want my daughter to go to mother-daughter banquets
31 alone or to go to strangers to learn about the birds and bees.
32 I'll get flowers for Mother's Day — not Memorial Day! I'll be
33 there when she goes on her first date and first prom and when

she gives the valedictorian speech . . . next week . . . Oh, God, I really miss my mom *(Picks up mother's picture)*, **even after five years, it still hurts so much. Why you, Mom? I'll never understand why somebody so good, somebody so caring . . . had to die and the world is so full of terrible people. It's been so hard, Mom . . . and Dad really tries. You'd really laugh if you could have seen the stuff he put in my lunchbox. And he is absolutely no good when it comes to personal problems . . . and my dating stories are straight from Alfred Hitchcock. And when he realizes he's a failure in the clenches, he brings in Grandma . . . and you know what she's like. She still thinks girls who shave their armpits are "hussies." She made me wear a crocheted shawl over my strapless gown. And when I graduate and get my diploma, I know you'd be there, Mom, if you could. I'm not really mad at you. It's just so unfair . . . but I'm going to do something about it, Mom, and I'll do it for both of us. Someday I'm going to be the best mom in the whole world.**

31

SCOPIN' CHICKS

Wonder what's keeping Jeff? He was supposed to meet me ten minutes ago. But Jeff never has had any sense of time. He thinks his Mickey Mouse hands are just on his watch to wave at him! Whew, look at that bunch of girls! Definitely Dallas Cowboy cheerleader material. The little one winked at me. Whoever said good things come in small packages must have wanted to find her in his stocking come Christmas morning.

I suppose all of these females are on their way to the movie. It's supposed to be a real tear-jerker. My sister and her friends love nothing better than a ten-Kleenex movie. She's always coming home saying, "It's a wonderful show; I cried all the way through it!" Women! Wow, look at those twins . . . talk about doubling your pleasure! Man, I've never seen so many hot babes! They're coming in packs. I wonder if there's some sort of beauty pageant in town? Or do you suppose they've always been here and I didn't know it? Well, I know it now! I hope Jeff doesn't rush; he'll be the kiss of death to this classy chick parade. Jeff just hasn't learned the secret of being cool around women. He stumbles, steps on their toes, gets tongue-tied and on a good day vomits! He needs lessons on understanding women — and who gives them? They have computer programs for everything else, but I have yet to see IBM crank out a "Ways to Not Bomb With Babes" disc.

Oh, no . . . be still my heart. It's a redhead . . . with freckles everywhere! Eyes as green as a bottle of Scope, and skin . . . skin as white as day-old marshmallows, and it covers everything. I'm going to have to sit down; I'm getting weak. Look how her lungs work . . . in and out, in and out. And Mother Nature sure put in just the right amount of yeast when she baked *those* buns! I wonder if she's all alone? Do you suppose she'd laugh if I went over and like actually spoke to her? My voice would probably squeak, or no words would come out, or I'd just stand there and gag. But nobody's around to witness my defeat . . . it wouldn't be public humiliation. Nobody would know but me, and the two thousand girlfriends she'd tell! I can live with that. Look, she's touching her ear lobe. I'd give a year's allowance for one little nibble on that left lobe. And look at her dainty, little fingers. I wonder if she'd run them through my hair if I promise to mow her lawn, do her geometry and give her my baseball card collection? Man, what a nose . . . turned up and so evenly centered in the middle of her face! Oh, no, she's smiling . . . at me! I think I'm going to have some sort of attack; I don't have this hormone thing completely figured out yet. Dad tried to explain it all to me, but I'm not sure he has a firm grasp on the subject either — Dad's a mortician!

Yep, she's coming this way. Sure wish I'd gargled. Oh, I just now remembered — I used my sister's deodorant and I'll bet it's *not* strong enough for a man!

What's that coming down the street? Oh, no, it's Jeff on his skateboard and he's wearing his Bugs Bunny ears. I'm a dead man. Yep, she sees him . . . knows he's yelling "What's up, Doc?" at me.

There she goes . . . little nose much higher in the air. But I did get a whiff of her perfume, so it wasn't a total loss. No, all-in-all it was a learning experience. Next week I'll return all duded up. I'll tell Jeff I'm going to the library; he'd never follow me there. Yep, this girl-watching thing sure beats the heck out of bird watching!

Dialogs

KEEP ON PUMPIN'

1 *CAST:* Ace and Spike
2 *AT RISE:* The two lifters are sitting on benches lifting hand
3 weights through the skit. On the floor are a gym bag, towels, etc.
4
5 **ACE: We really got the old biceps a thumpin' today, Spike.**
6 **SPIKE: Right on, Ace. My muscles are cryin' out for Icy Hot,**
7 **but I'm no baby. I'll just chomp down on a railroad tie**
8 **and keep a pumpin'!** *(He pumps with gusto.)*
9 **ACE: Spike, now that we're the toughest guys in**
10 **school . . . now that we can knock down a laundry truck**
11 **with our spit . . . now that our gym sweat can be sniffed**
12 **for two blocks — are we ready for the Big Test?**
13 **SPIKE:** *(Indian style)* **Right, Ke Mo Sabe. We pass-um muscle**
14 **test . . . now we pass Big Test of Fire.**
15 **ACE: Do we use caveman tactics and grab 'em by the hair**
16 **and drag 'em back to our caves?**
17 **SPIKE: Nah . . . because we have the muscles, we don't have**
18 **to use them. One look at these babies** *(Flexes biceps)* **and**
19 **women will follow us home like the little furry creatures**
20 **followed the Pied Piper.**
21 **ACE: I want women, not rats!**
22 **SPIKE: Take it easy, Ace, my man. Because the fairer sex**
23 ***loves* macho men, we're gonna get our pick of the litter.**
24 **We don't have to settle for crumbs; we can have cheese**
25 **cake.**
26 **ACE: Stop it, you're making me hungry and I want to talk**
27 **about women!**
28 **SPIKE: Ace, I can see you're gonna need a lot of help snaggin'**
29 **a prime babe.**
30 **ACE: I don't care if she's Miss America; I just want somebody**
31 **soft sitting by me at the movies.**
32 **SPIKE: You could keep taking your teddy bear!**
33 **ACE: Nah, I've outgrown Mr. Teddykins. They tried to make**

1 me buy a ticket for him last time!
2 SPIKE: How about a Barbie doll?
3 ACE: Negative . . . I want a breathin' doll — a babe — a hot
4 female machine!
5 SPIKE: Whoa, boy, calm down the old hormones. You have
6 to ease into these things.
7 ACE: But my biological clock is tickin'!
8 SPIKE: I knew I'd be sorry for teaching you to tell time on
9 your Mickey Mouse watch.
10 ACE: You promised I'd have girls falling at my feet if I worked
11 out every day.
12 SPIKE: And you will . . . be patient.
13 ACE: I'm gonna *be* a patient — in a mental ward — if I don't
14 start smellin' perfume, hearin' soft whispers in my ear,
15 buyin' Big Macs for two!
16 SPIKE: OK, OK, I guess you're ready.
17 ACE: EverReady, EverReady . . . we're talkin' nine lives here.
18 SPIKE: Calm down, man. Your hormonal computer is on
19 overload.
20 ACE: Right, I want to do some mega bytin' on some girl's ear
21 lobes!
22 SPIKE: I think I'm getting the picture — you're ready to
23 mingle with the opposite sex!
24 ACE: Mingle? I'm ready to grovel at the feet of anything
25 wearin' panty hose . . . even if there's a dog tag around
26 her neck!
27 SPIKE: I read you loud and clear.
28 ACE: I could always draw you a picture.
29 SPIKE: No drawings, please. We both got detention for
30 displaying our art work on the restroom wall.
31 ACE: It wasn't fair . . . old lady Sanders told us to let our
32 creative juices flow.
33 SPIKE: She probably didn't realize we'd be painting her
34 lifesize portrait above the urinals!
35 ACE: Who would have guessed it would take that much paint

1 **to draw a size eighteen bikini!**
2 **SPIKE: Whistler's Mother looked drab compared to our**
3 **masterpiece.**
4 **ACE: The world just wasn't ready for our kind of**
5 **genius . . . but back to *my* problem.**
6 **SPIKE: Oh, yes — the plan.**
7 **ACE: I'm all ears.**
8 **SPIKE: That's why you'll never be a painter. You didn't**
9 **sacrifice one of your old Dumbo flappers for the sake of**
10 **art!** *(Pulls on ACE's ear.)*
11 **ACE: A lot you know. Old lady Sanders stretched this left**
12 **lobe all the way to the office. Now, back to . . .** *(Said in the*
13 *voice of* Fantasy Island*'s Tattoo)* **the plan, Boss, the plan.**
14 **SPIKE: This is it: we're goin' cruisin' down Main Street in the**
15 **Bomber . . . all eight speakers on.**
16 **ACE: Yeah, yeah . . .**
17 **SPIKE: We'll slide into the Burger Bun wearin' our hottest**
18 **tank tops.**
19 **ACE: I'm with you, man.**
20 **SPIKE: We'll swagger past every booth, giving every chick**
21 **in the joint a chance to get an eyeful of our studly bods.**
22 **ACE: Then I can choose one?**
23 **SPIKE: Not so fast. You don't want to appear anxious — no**
24 **droolin' over the first babe who gives you the eye.**
25 **ACE: I was hopin' for *more* than her eye!**
26 **SPIKE: Always remember this, Ace: the world's a big**
27 **smorgasbord of women.**
28 **ACE: I'm ready for the entree . . . I'll even settle for leftovers.**
29 **SPIKE: The key to collecting hot chicks is to play it cool!**
30 **ACE: I'll remember — call me Mr. Refrigerator!**
31 **SPIKE: And one other thing . . .**
32 **ACE: There's more?**
33 **SPIKE:** *(As he gathers up his equipment)* **This is *very* important.**
34 **When we hit the showers, only wash one armpit.**
35 **ACE: Only one?**

1 **SPIKE: Yes, nothing turns the chicks on like the good, clean**
2 **hint of gym sweat.**
3 **ACE: Are you sure?**
4 **SPIKE: Nobody's invented Left Guard have they?**
5 **ACE: How did you get so wise, Spike?**
6 **SPIKE: It's a gift, Ace. Some can sing, others can play the**
7 **guitar. I was born with great biceps and *woman wise*.**
8 **Now, let's go put my knowledge to the test.**
9 **ACE: I hope I don't let you down, Spike. There's so much to**
10 **remember.**
11 **SPIKE: You'll do fine.** *(Puts towel around his neck, gets his gym*
12 *bag and starts to walk off.)* **Just keep your eye on *the master***
13 **and learn!** *(Exits.)*
14 **ACE:** *(Gathering up his gym stuff)* **This is it. The payback for**
15 **all that muscle strain. Must remember: be cool, ignore one**
16 **armpit . . . wow, I'm on my way. Good-bye ninety-nine-**
17 **pound weakling . . . hello, irresistible, macho stud!** *(Struts*
18 *off.)*
19
20
21
22
23
24
25
26
27
28
29
30
31
32
33
34
35

33

FINGERS DO THE WALKING

1 ***CAST:*** Kim and Kathy
2 ***AT RISE:*** Phone rings and Kim picks up her extension. Kathy is
3 on the other phone. A screen between them works well.
4
5 **KIM:** *(Picking up the phone)* **Hello.**
6 **KATHY:** *(Holding phone)* **Kim?**
7 **KIM: Kathy, I'm so glad you called. I tried to reach you earlier.**
8 **KATHY: I was out having a Coke with a guy . . . a very special**
9 **guy . . . a big hunk guy!**
10 **KIM: Really? I'm glad because I just had a call from a**
11 **gorgeous male specimen myself.**
12 **KATHY: Wow, we both scored! I knew it was going to be our**
13 **turn one of these days. You know what they say about**
14 **kissing frogs.**
15 **KIM: And we've kissed our share . . . kissed them till we got**
16 **wart lips! But that's all changing.**
17 **KATHY: Right! The "in" crowd all saw me seated with Mr.**
18 **Big Man on Campus. I just may be crossing over to the**
19 **other side — Popularity Island!**
20 **KIM: Do you actually have a date?**
21 **KATHY: Not exactly, but he mentioned meeting in the library**
22 **to work on our term papers together.**
23 **KIM: You work in the library, Kathy.**
24 **KATHY: I know . . . he mentioned that I could be a big help**
25 **with his reasearch. And guess what? He wrote my phone**
26 **number down on his palm! Imagine that! Hope he doesn't**
27 **wash his hands before he decides to call me!**
28 **KIM: Well, my call from a big wheel was really nice. He said**
29 **he'd been noticing me in geometry.**
30 **KATHY: Everyone notices you in geometry class, Kim. You're**
31 **the only one who knows what Mr. Chalkbutt is talking**
32 **about.**
33 **KIM: He said he'd been admiring my hair . . . wanted to know**

1 what kind of shampoo I use to make it so shiny. He said
2 he always had the urge to clip off a few curls to put in his
3 billfold for a keepsake!
4 KATHY: Wow! Sounds like a line from a soap opera.
5 KIM: I know, it gave me goosebumps.
6 KATHY: So did he ask you out?
7 KIM: No, but he did say it would be fun to do our geometry
8 assignments together.
9 KATHY: That's a start, and who wouldn't want to do geometry
10 with Ms. Einsteinbrain!
11 KIM: I really think he likes my hair better than my mind. He's
12 coming over tonight. I've got to shampoo and condition!
13 KATHY: Well, I'd better hang up . . . just in case Jason is
14 trying to call.
15 KIM: Jason?
16 KATHY: Yes, Jason Freemont — football hero, class
17 president, voted Most Likely to be President . . .
18 KIM: I can't believe it, Kathy!
19 KATHY: Well, thanks a lot for your vote of confidence. I
20 suppose you think I'm not good enough for Mr. Wonderful
21 . . . that he's slumming . . . that he only wants me to help
22 him with his research?
23 KIM: Oh, Kathy . . . I'm so sorry . . .
24 KATHY: You should be sorry. My best friend should be there
25 to bolster my courage . . . not rip my confidence to shreds!
26 KIM: It's not that, Kathy. It's just that we have a little problem.
27 KATHY: No, *you* have a little problem. You can't accept that
28 I'm moving up on the popularity scale . . . and you're
29 afraid I'll leave you behind!
30 KIM: No, Kathy, I'm proud of you. It's just that . . . well, you
31 see . . . um . . .
32 KATHY: Spit it out, Kim. You've never been at a loss for
33 words!
34 KIM: Kathy, this is going to hurt . . . believe me, I
35 know . . . but, Jason is coming to my house to work on

1 geometry!
2 KATHY: What?! I've only had him for an hour and already
3 you've stolen him!
4 KIM: I didn't steal him, Kathy. He's using both of us!
5 KATHY: I can't believe it! He was so sincere about noticing
6 me . . .
7 KIM: I'm sure he did notice you . . . *in the library* . . . and I'm
8 sure he did notice that you are very familiar with the
9 research tools!
10 KATHY: What a creep. He wants me to do his term paper and
11 you to coach him in geometry.
12 KIM: I think you're getting it!
13 KATHY: No, we're getting it — the shaft!
14 KIM: No, we aren't . . . because we caught on to his little game
15 before we humiliated ourselves.
16 KATHY: What's your plan?
17 KIM: Get over here quick. We're going to give Jason a call
18 he'll never forget. You'll be on the extension and we'll both
19 do the talking! He'll learn about hell having no fury like
20 *two* women scorned! When we get finished with him, he'll
21 never butter up a couple of smart females again to do his
22 assignments. In fact, he'll be very sorry he didn't just hire
23 himself a good tutor!
24 KATHY: I love it! Keep the phone line hot, I'm on my way!
25
26
27
28
29
30
31
32
33
34
35

NO SAFETY ZONE

1 *CAST:* Cassie and Fernando
2 *AT RISE:* Two students are sitting in desks in study hall.
3
4 **CASSIE: Did you see the fight down by room 205?**
5 **FERNANDO: Yeah, it was gang related everybody said.**
6 **CASSIE: I don't feel safe at school anymore.**
7 **FERNANDO: Nobody does . . . even in class.**
8 **CASSIE: Everywhere you look, knives . . .**
9 **FERNANDO: And guns.**
10 **CASSIE: Do you really think there are guns in our school?**
11 **FERNANDO: Wake up, Cassie. At times there are guns in**
12 **every school.**
13 **CASSIE: But some schools have those metal detectors . . . and**
14 **policemen on duty.**
15 **FERNANDO: Doesn't matter . . . where there's a weapon,**
16 **there's a way.**
17 **CASSIE: My mom thinks I should change to a private school.**
18 **FERNANDO: Lots of parents are taking their kids out of**
19 **public schools, and in a way you can't blame them.**
20 **CASSIE: Girls are almost afraid to walk down the halls alone.**
21 **FERNANDO: It's not any better for guys.**
22 **CASSIE: What's the answer?**
23 **FERNANDO: A lot of it must start at home. These kids need**
24 **more guidance and supervision and maybe love from their**
25 **parents.**
26 **CASSIE: It needs to start at a young age . . . it's probably too**
27 **late by the time they reach high school. Or maybe if**
28 **everyone just got more involved with extracurricular**
29 **activities — involvement . . . maybe that would cut down**
30 **on the violence in the schools.**
31 **FERNANDO: Maybe . . . Some of the really violent kids are**
32 **often victims of abuse or neglect.**
33 **CASSIE: Maybe they just need their egos restored in a positive**

1 way. Perhaps that could happen on the football field . . . or
2 on the wrestling mats.
3 FERNANDO: It might help, but in the meantime, the schools
4 need to do more to protect the innocent kids and teachers.
5 Get more hall monitors, parking lot supervisors, intercoms
6 in every classroom.
7 CASSIE: Right. I'm almost afraid to drive to school . . . afraid
8 that my car will be vandalized or I'll be attacked while
9 I'm getting in it.
10 FERNANDO: It used to be all students had to worry about
11 was their grades. Now it's personal safety as well.
12 CASSIE: I know. Maybe I'll give that private school some
13 more thought. Well, it's time for class, we'd better go.
14 FERNANDO: Come on, I'll walk you to class . . . just to be on
15 the *safe* side!
16
17
18
19
20
21
22
23
24
25
26
27
28
29
30
31
32
33
34
35

35

BUN WARMERS

1 *CAST:* Two football players
2 *AT RISE:* Two football players are sitting On-stage on a warped
3 bench. They are surrounded by helmets, water bottles, etc.
4
5 **1ST PLAYER: Man, I'm glad this is the last game of the season.**
6 **2ND PLAYER: Me, too. My buns are numb from keepin' this**
7 **bench warm.**
8 **1ST PLAYER: Numb? Mine are *paralyzed.* Last week I had a**
9 **three-inch splinter removed surgically without an**
10 **anesthetic!**
11 **2ND PLAYER: I think we're the only players who never have**
12 **grass stains.**
13 **1ST PLAYER: Who never put that black gunk under our eyes.**
14 **2ND PLAYER: Who never know the agony of defeat . . .**
15 **1ST PLAYER: Or hear that wonderful sound of our bones**
16 **snapping . . . crackling . . . popping.**
17 **2ND PLAYER: Man, I'd be great out there. Why, I eat a sack**
18 **of donuts every morning to give me quick energy.**
19 **1ST PLAYER: They're also giving you a beer gut!**
20 **2ND PLAYER: Naw . . . this is solid muscle . . . man of steel!**
21 **1ST PLAYER: I know. I've got muscles I've never thought of**
22 **using.**
23 **2ND PLAYER: Yeah, but most of them are in your brain.**
24 **1ST PLAYER: Ha! I'll have you know I made the Dean's List.**
25 **2ND PLAYER: Sure — the ten most wanted!**
26 **1ST PLAYER: I'd be a star if Coach would just wise up and**
27 **put me in.**
28 **2ND PLAYER: Well, you *did* run the wrong way that one time.**
29 **1ST PLAYER: Make a mistake *one* time and nobody forgets.**
30 **2ND PLAYER: Then last homecoming you got carried away**
31 **with your tackles.**
32 **1ST PLAYER: I'm trained to bring the opponents to the**
33 **ground . . . crush them . . . wipe them out!**

1 **2ND PLAYER: The *team* . . . not their head cheerleader!**
2 **1ST PLAYER: It's hard to tell . . . they were all wearing black**
3 **and orange.**
4 **2ND PLAYER: The way she filled out her letter sweater**
5 **should have been a *big* clue.**
6 **1ST PLAYER: She *was* the softest, sweetest-smelling tackle I**
7 **ever made. It was almost worth being terminally benched.**
8 **2ND PLAYER: It sure embarrassed your dad!**
9 **1ST PLAYER: Not as much as the time I had half a roll of**
10 **toilet paper hanging from the back of my helmet.**
11 **2ND PLAYER: I guess we just weren't cut out to be super**
12 **jocks.**
13 **1ST PLAYER: Yeah, but we do have athlete's foot!**
14 **2ND PLAYER: Look — Coach is coming our way!**
15 **1ST PLAYER: Naw, he just stepped off the field to spit.**
16 **2ND PLAYER: Whew! What if I'd get sent in and make a fool**
17 **of myself? How'd you feel after all those boo-boos?**
18 **1ST PLAYER: It was nothin' except for seeing Jill Samson**
19 **grinning at me and shakin' her big pompoms.**
20 **2ND PLAYER: Yeah, pompoms. We'd sure be socially dead if**
21 **we messed up out there.**
22 **1ST PLAYER: We're not exactly racking up popularity votes**
23 **sitting on this rotten bench.**
24 **2ND PLAYER: I don't know. Cindy Carter always smiles at**
25 **me during geometry.**
26 **1ST PLAYER: Smiles? She laughs out loud. Have you heard**
27 **some of your answers?**
28 **2ND PLAYER: Mr. Thomas makes me nervous when he talks**
29 **about isosceles triangles. The only kind of *sauce* I like is**
30 **hot fudge sauce or pizza sauce.**
31 **1ST PLAYER: You're hopeless. Uh-oh. Coach is waving us to**
32 **come in.**
33 **2ND PLAYER: I knew he'd need us. I can feel my energy level**
34 **rising.**
35 **1ST PLAYER: It's just your helmet strap. It's too tight on your**

1 **Adam's apple! Come on, I knew Coach would get tired to**
2 **seeing all of this raw talent wasted on a bench.**
3 **2ND PLAYER: We'll probably turn the game around.**
4 **1ST PLAYER: We're already ahead thirty-six points,**
5 **Hercules.**
6 **2ND PLAYER: Well, we'll just make it an over-powering**
7 **victory!**
8 **1ST PLAYER:** *(Sings in Mighty Mouse voice.)* **Here we come to**
9 **save the day!**
10 **2ND PLAYER: Let's be tough . . .**
11 **1ST PLAYER: Show no mercy . . .**
12 **2ND PLAYER: Be all we can be.**
13 **1ST PLAYER: Charge!** *(They run off making macho, grunting*
14 *noises. The scream of fans in the background.)*
15
16
17
18
19
20
21
22
23
24
25
26
27
28
29
30
31
32
33
34
35

TWO CAN KEEP A SECRET

1 *CAST:* Vicki and Erin
2 ***AT RISE:*** Vicki's On-stage calling to Erin, who joins her.
3
4 **VICKI: Hey, Erin, come over here quick before Shelly sees**
5 **you.**
6 **ERIN: What's up?**
7 **VICKI: What's up? You mean you haven't heard? I can't**
8 **believe it . . . and you the gossip editor for the *Tiger Tales*!**
9 **ERIN: Well?**
10 **VICKI: I probably shouldn't tell. I *was* sworn to secrecy.**
11 **ERIN: Since when has that stopped you?**
12 **VICKI: I'm sure I don't know what you mean. I can keep a**
13 **confidence as well as the next person.**
14 **ERIN: Who leaked the story of our super football hero, Brad**
15 **Taylor, cheating on Bonny Wilson? Who hid the tape**
16 **recorder in the boys' locker room and sold copies for three**
17 **bucks? Who played *Candid Camera* in the teachers' lounge**
18 **and played it at the Board of Education meeting?**
19 **VICKI: Oh, that was a good one.**
20 **ERIN: You got five teachers put on probation.**
21 **VICKI: Well, those little isolated incidents don't prove I can't**
22 **keep a secret.**
23 **ERIN: As well as the next blabber lips, you mean!**
24 **VICKI: I resent that remark . . . and just for that you'll have**
25 **to find out this tasty, delectable, juicy bit of scuttlebutt**
26 **yourself. You'll have to get your gossip tidbits the old**
27 **fashioned way: you'll have to *earn* them!**
28 **ERIN: Cool down, Vicki! I wasn't referring to you as "loose**
29 **lips" in a derogatory way!**
30 **VICKI: When you call somebody a blabber mouth, tall-tale**
31 **spreader, reputation ripper, gossip monger, I do *not***
32 **believe you are recommending them for a Girl Scout merit**
33 **award!**

1 ERIN: But I like that kind of person; some of my best friends
2 are snitches!
3 VICKI: Don't try to butter me up. I'll save my savory stories
4 for the *Tattler*.
5 ERIN: No, not my biggest competitor! That underground
6 school paper is taking over our reading public. If you have
7 something newsworthy, Vicki, you *must* share it with *my*
8 readers.
9 VICKI: Well . . .
10 ERIN: Please . . . I'll treat you to a banana split after geometry
11 class.
12 VICKI: Speaking of geometry . . . I didn't get around to doing
13 the assignment today . . .
14 ERIN: Here, be my guest . . . Xerox my paper. *(Hands it to her.)*
15 VICKI: Well, if you insist. My grade could use a boost.
16 ERIN: My gossip column could use a boost, too, so give.
17 VICKI: Well, it seems . . . Oh, by the way, could you mention
18 me in the column? I haven't had any good press lately.
19 ERIN: Oh, sure. I'll drop a little hint about your upcoming
20 pre-prom party.
21 VICKI: Oh, that'd be super. Now, where were we?
22 ERIN: Nowhere! About the story?
23 VICKI: Oh, of course, the story . . . well, I have it from a very
24 good source that . . .
25 ERIN: What source? We newspaper women like to have our
26 facts straight.
27 VICKI: Oh, I couldn't tell you who told me.
28 ERIN: Why not?
29 VICKI: I took an oath. Besides, it's not nice to tell who told
30 you something.
31 ERIN: It's not *nice* to fool Mother Nature! As for who told
32 you, only newspaper people have to protect their sources.
33 Since you're just a carrier, it's OK to tell all.
34 VICKI: Really?
35 ERIN: Sure. Think of it as your civic duty . . . your patriotic

1 **obligation.**
2 **VICKI: It is a little uncanny the way people turn to me with**
3 **little bits of dirt . . . about somebody else's life. I guess it's**
4 **sort of a gift, huh?**
5 **ERIN: Right! Some can play the piano, others sing like birds,**
6 **and you, Vicki, suck up gossip like a giant Kirby!**
7 **VICKI: And my mother's always telling me I have no talents!**
8 **Uh-oh, the bell . . . gotta get this geometry assignment run**
9 **off and get my buns to class. See ya.** *(Leaves.)*
10 **ERIN: Wait . . . you haven't told me the big story. Vicki, wait!**
11 **Well, lost another one. But I saved the price of a banana**
12 **split! Guess I was wrong; sometimes Vicki *can* keep a**
13 **secret!**
14
15
16
17
18
19
20
21
22
23
24
25
26
27
28
29
30
31
32
33
34
35

37

ADOPT A GRANDPARENT

1 *CAST:* Penny and Sue
2 *AT RISE:* The two girls are sitting in chairs in a waiting room at
3 a local resthome.
4
5 **PENNY: I don't know why I let you talk me into coming down**
6 **here. Why didn't we go to the mall or over to the malt shop?**
7 **SUE: We came to introduce you to a few of my other friends.**
8 **PENNY: I know all of your friends . . . the important ones,**
9 **anyway.**
10 **SUE: Not true. Some of my most important friends are here.**
11 **PENNY: I can't believe it! Everybody here is old. I hate old**
12 **people.**
13 **SUE: You don't even know any old people, Penny. It's time**
14 **you met some.**
15 **PENNY: If I didn't need the credit for my psychology class,**
16 **you'd never have talked me into this. Look at all those old**
17 **people . . . strapped in chairs . . . staring into space . . .**
18 **moaning . . . it's disgusting!**
19 **SUE: No, it isn't. They're just elderly, but they're still people.**
20 **They have feelings. And some of them can hear as well as**
21 **we can, so keep your voice down! Why don't you go over**
22 **and talk to some of them?**
23 **PENNY: No, they might touch me! Besides, they don't smell**
24 **good. This whole place stinks!**
25 **SUE: It's just a combination of Ben Gay and Polident. I want**
26 **to take you down to room 312 and introduce you to Lucy,**
27 **my adopted grandmother. She's a peach — so funny and**
28 **bubbly. She always has some funny stories to tell me about**
29 **the "good old days."**
30 **PENNY: I'd say it's been a looong time since any of these**
31 **people had good days.**
32 **SUE: That's why I come down here . . . to help make their days**
33 **a little better. I bring pictures . . . read to them. Once I**

1 brought my little niece and her puppy. They liked Polly,
2 but they loved the puppy!
3 PENNY: I can't believe you spend so much time here. Do you
4 get paid or at least get lots of extra credit?
5 SUE: No, I just started coming to see Lucy when my advisor
6 arranged for us to adopt grandparents. Then I saw how
7 lonely some of these people are. Some of them don't have
8 any family to visit them.
9 PENNY: Really?
10 SUE: Well, some have family . . . they just don't come to see
11 them.
12 PENNY: Maybe they're just uncomfortable around old
13 people . . . sick people.
14 SUE: That's no excuse! These people didn't ask to be old or
15 sick . . . or to be dumped here then forgotten by their
16 relatives.
17 PENNY: I guess not. Sue, I said I didn't know any old
18 people . . . that's not exactly true. My grandfather's old,
19 and he's in a nursing home, too.
20 SUE: Do you ever see him?
21 PENNY: Only on Christmas and sometimes in July on his
22 birthday. He had a stroke and can't talk very well . . . and
23 one side of his face is droopy.
24 SUE: But I'll bet he still knows you, doesn't he?
25 PENNY: Yes, but I can't understand him. It's embarrassing
26 to watch him try to talk and not be able to. He was a
27 lawyer, won hundreds of cases, and now he can't say a
28 sentence that you can understand. But he does always
29 look happy to see us. Maybe I should try to talk Mom into
30 going more often. He's probably lonesome . . . like some of
31 these people.
32 SUE: I'll bet he'd like that.
33 PENNY: Maybe we can go tomorrow and take him a present.
34 What do they like?
35 SUE: Company's what they like best . . . to know somebody

1 **remembers them and cares.**
2 **PENNY: I never thought about that. I just always thought**
3 **how hard it was for me . . . not how much it might mean**
4 **to Granddad.** *(Gets up.)* **Come on, let's go meet your adopted**
5 **grandmother . . . and as we go along, introduce me to a**
6 **few of your friends.**
7 **SUE:** *(Gets up.)* **Sure thing, Penny. You're going to get your**
8 **class credit, and you're going to meet some very interesting**
9 **people.**
10 **PENNY: I can't wait; let's go.**
11
12
13
14
15
16
17
18
19
20
21
22
23
24
25
26
27
28
29
30
31
32
33
34
35

GIRLS COME IN ALL SHAPES

1 *CAST:* Mike and Foober
2 *AT RISE:* The two boys are sitting on beach towels, wearing shades.
3
4 **MIKE: Isn't this great? . . . a whole day at the beach.**
5 **FOOBER: Yeah, no homework, no job, no ball practice.**
6 **MIKE: It's great. We don't have to strain anything.**
7 **FOOBER: Except our eyes . . . take a look at those babes!**
8 **MIKE: Calm down, Foob, you've got to pace yourself. We're**
9 **here for the whole day, and you can't short circuit on the**
10 **first little jolt of big voltage.**
11 **FOOBER: Zzzttt!** *(Acts like he's getting an electric shock.)* **I like**
12 **this shock treatment.**
13 **MIKE: You're going to see a lot of girls . . . a lot of bikinis . . . a**
14 **lot of skin.**
15 **FOOBER: Oh, boy. I like skin!**
16 **MIKE: Foober!**
17 **FOOBER: Right, Mike . . . pace myself. But, but, did you see**
18 **the . . . and the way she . . .**
19 **MIKE: Foob, you're drooling!**
20 **FOOBER: So?**
21 **MIKE: Nobody's going to pay attention to a guy with spit**
22 **dribbling down his chin. None of the *hot* babes anyway.**
23 **FOOBER: They're *all* hot. It's one hundred ten degrees today.**
24 **MIKE: Remember our little talk, Foob?**
25 **FOOBER: Oh, yeah. Forget the clown act . . . time to grow**
26 **up . . . act my age . . . no scratching.**
27 **MIKE: That's the one.**
28 **FOOBER: My Grandma still gives me the same speech every**
29 **week before I go to Sunday school.**
30 **MIKE: Well, *listen* this time. We don't want to be shot down**
31 **by these beach bunnies because you keep acting like Lou**
32 **Costello.**
33 **FOOBER: He's on first . . . who's on second!**

1 **MIKE: See? That's what I'm talking about! Girls don't like**
2 **that.**
3 **FOOBER: Not true. Girls are always laughing when I'm**
4 **around.**
5 **MIKE: *At* you. That's my point! So today, forget the dork**
6 **act . . . be a *man*!**
7 **FOOBER: Be a man . . . I can do that! I did shave those three**
8 **manly hairs off my chin. I did use a deodorant made for**
9 **a man. You've got it, Mike. I'm turning a new page, taking**
10 **off the old mask, getting rid of my bag of tricks! Except**
11 **the whoopie cushion. I'm very attached to the whoopie**
12 **cushion. If you take it away, it would be like when Mommy**
13 **took my blankie!**
14 **MIKE: Keep the whoopie cushion . . . just don't use it today.**
15 **Wet, shapely buns and whoopie cushions just don't get it!**
16 **FOOBER: I'm not so sure. Imagine the surprised look, the . . .**
17 **MIKE: Foober!**
18 **FOOBER: OK, OK, I'll retire the whoopie cushion . . . but it's**
19 **a heck of an ice breaker.**
20 **MIKE: Well, there's no ice here today . . . just a lot of warm,**
21 **sweaty, steamy . . .**
22 **FOOBER: Hey, hey . . .** *(Fans MIKE)* **calm down the old**
23 **hormones, Mike. Pace yourself, remember!**
24 **MIKE: I almost forgot myself . . . and we don't want to seem**
25 **too anxious.**
26 **FOOBER: Play hard to get, huh?**
27 **MIKE: Sort of . . . but, of course, we *do* want to get *got*!**
28 **FOOBER: You said it, Mike. I wonder how long it will take**
29 **to snag a prize chick?**
30 **MIKE: Not too long. Take a look at that group — now that's**
31 **prime-time viewing.**
32 **FOOBER: I wonder how Neilsen would rate them?**
33 **MIKE: On a scale of one to ten — twelves all the way!**
34 **FOOBER: Except for the one in back. Her buns O.D.'d on the**
35 **yeast . . . hope I don't get stuck with something like that!**

1 **MIKE: Look, there aren't many guys here. I'd say we can have**
2 **first choice — dip off the cream.**
3 **FOOBER: Just so I don't have to get the cottage cheese . . . you**
4 **know, those girls with hail damage on their thighs.**
5 **MIKE: It's called cellulite, Foob, and I guarantee you, you**
6 **won't have to get close to cellulite today.**
7 **FOOBER: Do you promise?**
8 **MIKE: If you get stuck with some female with chunky**
9 **drumsticks today, I will personally do your homework for**
10 **the next month.**
11 **FOOBER: Really? It'd kill my mother, of course. She has a**
12 **weak heart . . . but it'd be worth it to make the honor roll!**
13 **MIKE: Don't count your chicks . . . unless you're counting**
14 **those tanned, sexy volleyball players over there. You won't**
15 **be spending time with any female who isn't cover girl**
16 **material.**
17 **FOOBER: But if my cover girl *really* covers the magazine . . . if**
18 **it takes six pages to do a centerfold . . . you'll be doing my**
19 **assignments through May, right?**
20 **MIKE: Right.**
21 **FOOBER: Wow, take a look over there . . . twins! I'm taking**
22 **a double take.** *(Looks twice.)* **Shall we reel them in for a**
23 **double date?** *(Casts and reels.)*
24 **MIKE: Watch it, Foob. Consider this a nerd alert.** *(Throws water*
25 *in his face.)*
26 **FOOBER: Thanks, Mike. I needed that. Guess that means the**
27 **twins are out, huh?**
28 **MIKE: Right. No use hitting on them. You'd never be able to**
29 **contain yourself. You'd be *doubling* over, buying *double-***
30 ***dip* cones, *doubling* your fun . . . and before I knew it,**
31 **you'd be draggin' out the old whoopie cushion.**
32 **FOOBER: You're a wise man, Mike Pierce. Oh, my**
33 **gosh . . . don't look . . . save your eyesight. It's two of our**
34 **least favorite teachers — Miss Franklin and Ms.**
35 **Thomas . . . in, I guess you'd call them, swimsuits. Oh, no,**

1 they're waving at us!
2 MIKE: Pretend you're reading. That'll impress them.
3 FOOBER: Yeah, sure. Like *Playboy* is on our assigned
4 reading list!
5 MIKE: If they park by us, we're doomed.
6 FOOBER: Whew, we're off the hook. They're going over by
7 the lifeguard . . . poor sap . . . they'll probably make him
8 diagram sentences when he's not saving damsels in
9 distress.
10 MIKE: What a break . . . for us, not the lifeguard.
11 FOOBER: Did you get a look at those bods?
12 MIKE: No, I was afraid to risk it without eye protection!
13 FOOBER: But ya gotta admire them. It takes guts to poke
14 bodies like those in XXL swimsuits and head for the beach!
15 MIKE: Now they probably looked great in swimsuits when
16 they were young.
17 FOOBER: When they were young, John the Baptist provided
18 the swimwear!
19 MIKE: Well, forget about them and get back to concentrating
20 on fine, tan, curvy bodies.
21 FOOBER: Yeah, with buns of aluminum.
22 MIKE: Steel, Foob, buns of steel!
23 FOOBER: Right, my mind's still mixed up. It keeps trying to
24 erase that awful sight from my memory . . . of seeing two
25 marshmallow-legged school marms in Esther Williams
26 suits. My stomach is still queasy . . . hope it hasn't ruined
27 my lunch.
28 MIKE: Nothing could ruin your lunch, Foob. You ate while
29 Tommy was throwing up in his lunch tray; you ate while
30 Julio was . . .
31 FOOBER: Yeah, yeah. But those two letting it all hang out
32 can even get to an iron gut like mine.
33 MIKE: Well, your guts are in for a treat now. Look at those
34 two prize chicks heading our way.
35 FOOBER: Hey, they're giving us that old you'll-do-till-

1 Stallone-gets-here look!
2 MIKE: Yep, they're taking the bait . . .
3 FOOBER: What bait? We weren't planning to fish.
4 MIKE: The shades, the biceps, the smile . . .
5 FOOBER: Oh, that bait! Yeah, maybe I should flex a couple
6 of times. The size of my muscles might impress them.
7 MIKE: Forget it, Foob. They've seen jelly beans.
8 FOOBER: Hey! I've been lifting a year to get these babies.
9 MIKE: Yeah, lifting your fork . . . to your face!
10 FOOBER: Well, it's working. They're putting their towels
11 pretty close. And the blonde's smiling . . . at me!
12 MIKE: This is it, Foob, we came, we saw . . .
13 FOOBER: And we've *been* conquered!
14 MIKE: What do you mean?
15 FOOBER: The jaws sisters are on their way back. I'm talking
16 teachers in latex.
17 MIKE: They're yelling something . . . oh, no . . . they want to
18 share their lunch with us. We're ruined!
19 FOOBER: Our "stud biscuit" image is shot to . . .
20 MIKE: The girls are moving away . . . heading for the
21 lifeguard.
22 FOOBER: Sure, they felt the ground moving from the running
23 of little teacher feet. They thought it was an earthquake.
24 MIKE: Lunch with our teachers . . . what a treat!
25 FOOBER: Kiss of death to us socially. I hope they don't ask
26 us to rub lotion on their backs.
27 MIKE: Our day's shot! Our life's shot! We'll never live this
28 down.
29 FOOBER: All this sunburn for nothing.
30 MIKE: Wasted money on a new aftershave.
31 FOOBER: But we will have the chance to do some major
32 kissing up.
33 MIKE: And your grade could use the boost.
34 FOOBER: My grades don't need any help . . . not for the next
35 month at least.

1 **MIKE: What do you mean?**
2 **FOOBER: I mean *you'll* be doing all of my assignments. I'm**
3 **taking the next four weeks off!**
4 **MIKE: Wait, this doesn't count!**
5 **FOOBER: You said if I got stuck with cellulite today, you'd**
6 **do my homework for the next month . . . and if that isn't**
7 **cellulite heading our way . . .**
8 **MIKE: OK, OK. It's a rip-off, but a deal's a deal.**
9 **FOOBER: This isn't going to turn out so bad . . . make A's for**
10 **a month and get brownie points with my grandma. They're**
11 **both in her ladies' club.**
12 **MIKE: And they've *got* to be good cooks.**
13 **FOOBER: They didn't get those thighs eating carrot sticks.**
14 **MIKE: They've got two big food baskets.**
15 **FOOBER: That's not all they've got that's big!**
16 **MIKE: We can feed our peanut butter sandwiches to the**
17 **fishes.**
18 **FOOBER: Mike, maybe we need to change our bait next time**
19 **we come to the beach . . . cause if this is what we're always**
20 **going to catch, let's just let our fishing license expire!**
21
22
23
24
25
26
27
28
29
30
31
32
33
34
35

IT'S ONLY A GAME

1 *CAST:* Tonya and Eric
2 *AT RISE:* Eric is staring at the TV screen. Tonya is trying to pull
3 him away from it.
4
5 **TONYA: Come on, Eric, I don't want to watch another football**
6 **game. Let's go to the mall or the show.**
7 **ERIC: No can do, Tonya. This isn't just *any* game, you know.**
8 **TONYA: Is it the Superbowl . . . the playoffs?**
9 **ERIC: No, but it's important.**
10 **TONYA: Do you have a big bet on the outcome?**
11 **ERIC: You know I'm busted. Spent my last dime on that**
12 **cheeseburger we split at Wendy's last night.**
13 **TONYA: Thanks. I expected a little more when you said we**
14 **were going out to dinner.**
15 **ERIC: Can I help it if I'm a little short of money this month?**
16 **TONYA: Couldn't you be working now instead of watching**
17 **this game? Couldn't you have worked Monday night and**
18 **made time and a half?**
19 **ERIC: What? And miss Monday night football?! Tonya,**
20 **thoughts like that give me hypertension. I could miss my**
21 **American lit class, Sunday school, monthly haircut or even**
22 **Saturday morning cartoons, but *not* Monday night**
23 **football!**
24 **TONYA: I give up! Everybody is right: you like football better**
25 **than you like me.**
26 **ERIC: Now, Tonya, that's not true . . . not exactly true,**
27 **anyway.**
28 **TONYA:** *(Weeping)* **I'm coming in second to a pigskin!**
29 **ERIC: Now, now, Tonya, quit weeping. It's hard for me to**
30 **hear the announcer.**
31 **TONYA:** *(Crying louder)* **I should have fallen in love with a**
32 **musician, an outlaw, a mortician.**
33 **ERIC: Nobody's perfect. We all have our little flaws.**

1 TONYA: Not Fred Carter!
2 ERIC: Oh, no, not the Fred Carter story again. I know, I know,
3 he was crazy about you. He had millions in the bank. He
4 named a petting zoo after you. He had Tonya written
5 fifteen times in the sky in colored smoke.
6 TONYA: And he didn't like football!
7 ERIC: Then why did you drop him like a rotten egg at a bunny
8 hunt and choose "yours truly"?
9 TONYA: At times like this I don't have the foggiest idea.
10 ERIC: Maybe it was because Fred looked like Frankenstein's
11 grandma, or maybe it was Freddy's Woody Woodpecker
12 laugh!
13 TONYA: It's what's on the inside that counts.
14 ERIC: Right . . . and inside Fred's bank balance was a lot of
15 zeroes!
16 TONYA: You know I'm not a golddigger. Or I'd be covered
17 with mink and be eating the best cuisine instead of
18 splitting Big Macs!
19 ERIC: That's what I like about you, Tonya. You're such a
20 good sport.
21 TONYA: Don't call me that. I hate anything that has to do
22 with sports!
23 ERIC: If you'd just pay attention, you'd learn to like the game.
24 TONYA: Nothing could make me like watching grown men
25 fighting for two hours over a stupid little ball.
26 ERIC: Think of it as a drama, Tonya. You love Shakespeare.
27 TONYA: Something tells me that the Bard was not referring
28 to a dumb jock with a football under his arm when he
29 said, "To be or not to be."
30 ERIC: Maybe not, but I *do* think it was Joe Montana's mother
31 who said, "Out, damned spot" when she was washing his
32 uniform!
33 TONYA: Talking to you is hopeless, Eric.
34 ERIC: You're right, so why don't you go fix us a couple of hot
35 dogs.

1 **TONYA: I don't know why I waste my time on a sports-**
2 **minded, football-addicted moron.**
3 **ERIC: But I have these sexy eyes, remember?**
4 **TONYA: I wouldn't know. They're never taken off the TV set.**
5 **ERIC: And don't forget my buns of steel!**
6 **TONYA: Your buns have been Elmered to that couch cushion**
7 **since football season started.**
8 **ERIC: Yeah, but what a treat to look forward to when the**
9 **season ends. Lucky for you basketball doesn't turn me on!**
10 **TONYA: The only thing that turns you on is somebody**
11 **running down the field in a Bears uniform.**
12 **ERIC: Not true . . . I'm a Raiders fan. I'm only kidding, Tonya.**
13 **I'd much rather look at you than this game.**
14 **TONYA: Oh, Eric, really?**
15 **ERIC: Sure. You're beautiful, Tonya. There's only one little**
16 **thing that would make you look better.**
17 **TONYA: A little gloss added to my lips?**
18 **ERIC: No . . . a hotdog in each hand . . . before the second half**
19 **of the game starts!**
20
21
22
23
24
25
26
27
28
29
30
31
32
33
34
35

40

SPLITTING UP

1 *CAST:* Erin and Cheryl
2 *AT RISE:* Erin enters. Cheryl is sitting at her desk.
3
4 **ERIN: What's up, Cheryl? Your mom said you weren't feeling**
5 **well.**
6 **CHERYL: Oh, I'm not *sick* sick . . . just heartsick.**
7 **ERIN: That's the worst kind of illness. You're missing your**
8 **dad, aren't you?**
9 **CHERYL: Uh-huh. I helped him pack last night and load up**
10 **his pickup for the last time. Buddy wouldn't even speak**
11 **to him; he blames Dad for the divorce.**
12 **ERIN: Who do you blame? Your mom?**
13 **CHERYL: I did at first. I thought if she'd just be a little nicer**
14 **to him he'd stay. But I finally realized it wasn't going to**
15 **work. They fought over everything — what kind of dog**
16 **food Elmo liked best, who had to take Buddy to T-ball**
17 **practice, who wasted most of the money. They even fought**
18 **over which toilet paper was softest!**
19 **ERIN: I know, once they fall out of love, they hate everything**
20 **about each other. My folks stayed together too long — for**
21 **me and my sister. It was much better when they split.**
22 **CHERYL: Really? But didn't you miss your father?**
23 **ERIN: Sure, but when I do see him he's laughing.**
24 **CHERYL: I haven't heard my dad laugh for a long time.**
25 **ERIN: He will . . . after a while. So will your mom and so will**
26 **you.**
27 **CHERYL: I doubt that. I wonder what makes them fall out**
28 **of love?**
29 **ERIN: Lots of stuff — like money, kids, bills, jobs and**
30 **household chores. Mom says it's a stressful world out there**
31 **for adults and for us not to be in such a hurry to grow up.**
32 **CHERYL: That's what Dad says: to stay a kid as long as I**
33 **can. I'm really going to miss him.**

ERIN: Remember, he's only a phone call away, and you'll see him on weekends and vacations.

CHERYL: But it won't be the same.

ERIN: No, it'll never be the same, but in some ways it'll be better. Better than all the hatred and bitterness. Who knows, your folks might even become friends again in time . . . mine did.

CHERYL: I don't see that happening.

ERIN: Time heals a lot. Now, put on a smile, we're going out for banana splits.

CHERYL: I couldn't swallow one . . . that's Dad's favorite treat.

ERIN: Then we'll make it a hot fudge sundae. I won't take no for an answer.

CHERYL: OK, I need to get out of this house. It's so quiet . . . so hollow.

ERIN: It'll come to life again, so will you and your folks. You'll see.

CHERYL: I guess you're right. But I'll tell you one thing, Cheryl, when I get married I'm going to be very, very sure it'll last. I never want to put my kids through the agony of divorce.

CON-*GRAD*-U-LATIONS

1 ***CAST:*** Two male graduates
2 ***AT RISE:*** Two seniors come On-stage . . . in front of the curtain
3 works well. They are carrying caps and gowns. During the skit
4 they put them on.
5
6 **1ST GRAD: Well, this is it. We're finally graduating.**
7 **2ND GRAD: It wasn't easy. I just barely squeezed by in**
8 **American history. I passed by two points.**
9 **1ST GRAD: I heard you singing "The National Anthem" as**
10 **old lady Duke was grading your final.**
11 **2ND GRAD: Yeah, and I had my hand across my heart and**
12 **Old Glory tied around my back like a Superman cape!**
13 **1ST GRAD: It must have worked. You're Diploma Bait now.**
14 **You can start dating smart chicks instead of ones who still**
15 **eat paste.**
16 **2ND GRAD: That's right! I can go with the type of girl who**
17 **reads above the See-Spot-Run level.**
18 **1ST GRAD: Don't go too high. Remember, you're still in the**
19 **See-Jane-Jump series yourself.**
20 **2ND GRAD: Hey, I made A's on every book report I handed in.**
21 **1ST GRAD: Let's see . . . in twelve years that would be three!**
22 **And then you read the comic version.**
23 **2ND GRAD: Wrongo. I suffered through the video of *Hamlet*.**
24 **1ST GRAD: Yeah, but Minnie Mouse saying "To be or not to**
25 **be" loses some of the culture.**
26 **2ND GRAD: You want culture . . . get a six-pack of Dannon.**
27 **1ST GRAD: Well, it's all behind us now: book reports, pep**
28 **assemblies, principal's office, detention . . .**
29 **2ND GRAD: And the world is out there awaiting our arrival.**
30 **We're adults now . . . mature, educated humanoids!**
31 **1ST GRAD: Masters of our destiny . . .**
32 **2ND GRAD: We know *all* there is to know.**
33 **1ST GRAD: Our brains are so chucked full of trivia they're**

1 **ready to explode like a ripe zit!**
2 **2ND GRAD: No more rules . . . freedom!**
3 **1ST GRAD: We're free to forget childish curfews.**
4 **2ND GRAD: Free to date the kind of women we can't bring**
5 **home to Mommy!**
6 **1ST GRAD: Right . . . we're entering the age of fast cars, fast**
7 **foods and fast . . .**
8 **BOTH: *Women!*** *(Do a weird handshake.)*
9 **2ND GRAD: College dames are so worldly . . . so ripe for the**
10 **picking.**
11 **1ST GRAD: Can we pluck as many as we want, or is there a**
12 **limit?**
13 **2ND GRAD: Don't worry . . . there'll be plenty of women to go**
14 **around . . . and around and around . . .**
15 **1ST GRAD: Stop it. You're making me dizzy. I'm ready to**
16 **march down the aisle, get my diploma and head for the**
17 **Halls of Ivy.**
18 **2ND GRAD: I can't wait to get away from my mom's watchful**
19 **eye . . . wear the same underwear two days . . . drink**
20 **straight from the milk carton.**
21 **1ST GRAD: Leave the lid off the toothpaste and Jiffy jar.**
22 **2ND GRAD: Be able to manage my own money.**
23 **1ST GRAD: Yeah . . . Wait! What money?**
24 **2ND GRAD: Hey, that's right. Will my old man still give me**
25 **an allowance once I'm college material?**
26 **1ST GRAD: Will my mom still slip me twenty bucks . . . *if* I**
27 **should find a sweet, young thing who's good enough for**
28 **her baby boy?**
29 **2ND GRAD: And what if I need to borrow a car or have my**
30 **oil changed?**
31 **1ST GRAD: Who's gonna do our laundry? Who's gonna**
32 **correct my spelling and type my term papers? Who'll**
33 **straighten up my checking account?**
34 **2ND GRAD: Maybe we can find a girlfriend to do all that stuff.**
35 **1ST GRAD: I don't want to go with a girl dumb enough to be**

1 **a doormat.**
2 **2ND GRAD: Right. It looks like we've got a lot to learn this**
3 **summer.**
4 **1ST GRAD: Yeah, just when we thought getting a sheepskin**
5 **meant we knew everything!**
6 **2ND GRAD: It's not fair. We'll have to spend the whole**
7 **summer learning about fabric softeners, bookkeeping and**
8 **vacuum cleaners.**
9 **1ST GRAD: Maybe it's not gonna be worth it. We could trade**
10 **in our diplomas . . . stay kids forever!**
11 **2ND GRAD:** *("Pomp and Circumstance" is heard Off-stage.)* **Too**
12 **late . . . they're playing our song!**
13 **1ST GRAD: Today we become men.**
14 **2ND GRAD: It may not be all it's cracked up to be.**
15 **1ST GRAD: No backing out now. The march is playing . . . the**
16 **announcements were mailed . . . the gifts are rolling in.**
17 **2ND GRAD: I wish I'd enjoyed being a kid just a *little* longer.**
18 **1ST GRAD: Well, there *is* that graduation party tonight.**
19 **2ND GRAD: Right . . . I don't think we'll find too many adults**
20 **there.**
21 **1ST GRAD: Saved! Let's go . . . this conversation was getting**
22 **too deep.**
23 **2ND GRAD: Yeah, loosen up, buddy. We're about to become**
24 **high school graduates. Con-*grad*-u-lations!**
25 **1ST GRAD: Same to you.** *(They go through a long, "weird"*
26 *handshake ritual. The music gets louder, and they march off in*
27 *solemn, graduate style.)*
28
29
30
31
32
33
34
35

42

SHOP TILL WE DROP

1 *CAST:* Jennifer and Shelly
2 *AT RISE:* Both girls are cupping their hands around their eyes
3 staring at the audience as though they're looking into a locked
4 mall.
5
6 **JENNIFER:** *(Pointing)* **Look, Shelly, they've got racks and**
7 **racks of stuff to buy . . . and I've got money!**
8 **SHELLY: Hang in there, Jennifer. The mall will open in ten**
9 **minutes.**
10 **JENNIFER: I'm not sure I can wait ten minutes. We're talking**
11 **sidewalk sales . . . *bargains*!**
12 **SHELLY: Jen, I know you're a shopaholic, but you've got to**
13 **learn to have a little control . . . use a little bit of will power!**
14 **JENNIFER: Not a chance. It runs in our family. It's in the**
15 **genes. Oh, look at that rack of Pepy's. You see, my**
16 **grandma was a maniac shopping depressive; Aunt Phyllis**
17 **has charge cards in every big store in Texas. The females**
18 **in my family have shopping reunions . . . we give prizes**
19 **for the fullest shopping bags! Three of my cousins are in**
20 **therapy as we stand here waiting for them to open these**
21 **blasted doors.** *(Bangs on the air.)*
22 **SHELLY: Calm down, girl. You're going to need tranquilizers.**
23 **JENNIFER: I don't need anything but my credit card and for**
24 **everybody to stand out of my way!**
25 **SHELLY: You're hyperventilating, Jennifer. Take deep**
26 **breaths.**
27 **JENNIFER:** *(Breathes deeply.)* **It's no use. The only thing that**
28 **will alleviate the stress is to buy, buy, buy!**
29 **SHELLY: Let's concentrate on something else, Jennifer. Now,**
30 **why do most teenage girls come to the mall?**
31 **JENNIFER: To grab the most far-out earrings . . . to try on**
32 **the tightest jeans . . . to look for the coolest bikini.**
33

1 **SHELLY: Wrong! They come here because guys hang out in**
2 **malls.**
3 **JENNIFER: Guys hang out in malls? You're kidding!**
4 **SHELLY: Take a look . . . see that studly group over there?**
5 **JENNIFER: OK, I'll take my eyes off that rack of Minnie**
6 **Mouse T-shirts for a few seconds . . . but it hurts! Wow,**
7 **guys! I recognize a couple of them. We're talking lettermen!**
8 **SHELLY: Right, and they do not come here to buy Nikes on**
9 **sale. They come to scope the chicks!**
10 **JENNIFER: You mean they've always been here?**
11 **SHELLY: Hiding right behind your Visa and MasterCard.**
12 **JENNIFER: You mean if I'd been looking up from the sale**
13 **racks, I might have made eye contact with a Tom Cruise-**
14 **type guy?**
15 **SHELLY: It's possible, but it'll never happen with you in**
16 **combat with all the other early-bird shoppers.**
17 **JENNIFER: I would like to give that group of guys the once**
18 **over . . . you know, window shop . . . but I'm not sure I can**
19 **pull myself away from the red-light specials.**
20 **SHELLY: You won't have to go cold turkey. Just gradually**
21 **back off from the sale bins, ignore the check-out counters,**
22 **keep your checkbook in your purse.**
23 **JENNIFER: You don't know what you're asking!**
24 **SHELLY: You can do it, Jen. Take one more look at that guy**
25 **in the blue sweater: eyes that would melt a Hershey bar,**
26 **buns that should be chiseled on Mount Rushmore.**
27 **JENNIFER: Where? Where?**
28 **SHELLY: Over there, and he's looking your way.**
29 **JENNIFER: Oh, and I was in such a big hurry to be first in**
30 **line when the mall opened I forgot to put on any make-up**
31 **or brush my hair. I forgot to gargle, too.**
32 **SHELLY: He can't tell if your breath is springtime fresh from**
33 **that distance, but you might want to comb your hair and**
34 **put on a little lip gloss. Oh, look, they're opening the mall.**
35 **Let's go look at that table of purses.**

JENNIFER: Out of my way. I'm heading for the ladies' lounge.

SHELLY: But all the good stuff will be picked over when you get back.

JENNIFER: I don't think so. You go ahead and shop all you want, Shelly . . . have fun! Here's my credit card. I think I'll wander around in the middle of the mall. I've been ignoring that area too long, and I think that's where all the *really* good stuff's at!

43

DESIGNATED DRIVER

1 *CAST:* Patrick and Mike
2 *AT RISE:* Mike is putting on his coat to leave the party, and Patrick
3 stops him.
4
5 **PATRICK: Where are you heading, Mike?**
6 **MIKE: I'm splittin'.**
7 **PATRICK: Who's driving you?**
8 **MIKE: You're looking at my chauffeur . . . James to you!**
9 **PATRICK: You can't drive . . . you drank too much tonight.**
10 **MIKE: Nah, I didn't have so much, and I ate a lot. I'm OK.**
11 **PATRICK: No way, Mike. I'll take you home. I'm a designated**
12 **driver tonight. We'll come back and get your car tomorrow.**
13 **MIKE: Nah, the old man would blow a gasket if I left the ZX.**
14 **I'm fine, don't worry.**
15 **PATRICK: That's what Keith thought.**
16 **MIKE: That was just a fluke. It'd never happen to me.**
17 **PATRICK: I'm sure Keith felt the same way, and you saw his**
18 **family at the funeral . . . and his friends.**
19 **MIKE: God, I miss Keith. I stop off and see his mom from time**
20 **to time. I don't think she's ever going to be the same.**
21 **PATRICK: Wait here. I'll get Rick to follow in your car. He's**
22 **the D.D. for his group.**
23 **MIKE: You two are regular little martyrs . . . little Johns of**
24 **Arc.**
25 **PATRICK: Not at all. It was just my turn to drink Pepsi. I**
26 **want to see all of my friends tomorrow . . . alive.**
27 **MIKE: OK, OK. It's not necessary, but I know the old "friends**
28 **don't let friends" bit. And I wouldn't want you to lose your**
29 **Good Samaritan badge because of me.**
30 **PATRICK: Great . . . I'll go get Rick.**
31 **MIKE: Patrick?**
32 **PATRICK: Yeah?**
33 **MIKE: Thanks.**

IT'S BEEN FUN, BUT . . .

1 *CAST:* Gentra and Scott
2 *AT RISE:* Gentra is sitting on a bench. Scott approaches to join her.
3
4 **GENTRA: Here comes Scott. It's going to be hard, but I've**
5 **got to break it off . . . mustn't weaken!** *(To SCOTT)* **Hi,**
6 **Scott, I'm so glad you could meet me.**
7 **SCOTT:** *(Aside to audience)* **She wouldn't be so glad to see me**
8 **if she knew I was going to dump her like last week's**
9 **garbage.** *(To GENTRA)* **Hi, Gentra, let's sit down. I needed**
10 **to talk to you, too.**
11 **GENTRA:** *(Aside)* **Oh, no, he's probably going to ask me to the**
12 **prom or declare his undying love for me. I have that kind**
13 **of effect on every male I date.** *(To SCOTT)* **You sound so**
14 **serious, Scott. I hope everything is OK.**
15 **SCOTT:** *(Aside)* **OK? Her life will never be OK again. She's**
16 **about to lose the best catch in this school. She can say**
17 **good-bye to dating Mr. Popularity!** *(To GENTRA)*
18 **Everything's just fine. Did you do OK on the chemistry**
19 **test?**
20 **GENTRA:** *(Aside)* **Of course he'd mention chemistry. It's so**
21 **pathetic when there's one-sided chemistry. I can tell he's**
22 **so lovesick. I wish I didn't have this fatal attraction . . . it's**
23 **a curse.** *(To SCOTT)* **Oh, yes. I made my usual A. How did**
24 **you do?**
25 **SCOTT:** *(Aside)* **She makes A's OK, but by being Ms. Kiss-up,**
26 **not by studying. I'm going to date an airhead next.** *(To*
27 *GENTRA)* **I got an A, too. It was easy. What did you want**
28 **to talk to me about, Gentra?**
29 **GENTRA:** *(Aside)* **Here it comes. I hope he doesn't break down**
30 **and embarrass himself.** *(To SCOTT)* **I wanted to talk about**
31 **our relationship. We've been going together for two**
32 **months now.**
33 **SCOTT:** *(Aside)* **Only two months? It seems like a lifetime. I'll**

1 **bet she's going to ask for my class ring. No way!** *(To*
2 *GENTRA)* **Yes, we've become good friends, haven't we?**
3 **GENTRA:** *(Aside)* **I'd better cut him off now, before he wants**
4 **to take the friendship another step.** *(To SCOTT)* **That's it**
5 **exactly, Scott. We're really good friends, but . . .**
6 **SCOTT:** *(Aside)* **Oh, no. She wants *more* than friendship. I**
7 **don't even want friendship with her. She acts like my**
8 **mother. I'm afraid to leave vegetables on my plate when**
9 **we eat dinner out!** *(To GENTRA)* **Right, but that's not**
10 **enough — is that what you wanted to say?**
11 **GENTRA:** *(Aside)* **Oh, no, he wants to push this into a**
12 **permanent relationship! It would be like becoming serious**
13 **with my dentist.** *(To GENTRA)* **Not exactly. I mean, I think**
14 **friendship sometimes is enough . . . sometimes it's too**
15 **much!**
16 **SCOTT:** *(Aside)* **Oh, dear, she's heard that I'm going to drop**
17 **her and she's saving face. Oh, well, I'm a big enough man**
18 **to let her protect her precious image.** *(To GENTRA)* **I agree,**
19 **Gentra. Our friendship has become a burden . . . to both**
20 **of us. What say we just end it now?**
21 **GENTRA:** *(Aside)* **Oh, he's heartbroken! I knew it . . . why was**
22 **I born with this power to crush guys' hearts? He's being**
23 **so brave, I'll try to make it easy for him.** *(To SCOTT)* **Oh,**
24 **Scott, you're right, of course. Some things just weren't**
25 **meant to be . . . like Romeo and Juliet, Scarlet and Rhett.**
26 **SCOTT:** *(Aside)* **What a cover-up. Tomorrow she'll be blabbing**
27 **all over the school how she dumped me.** *(To GENTRA)*
28 **Let's just part friends. Have a good life, Gentra.** *(Hugs her.)*
29 **GENTRA:** *(Aside)* **He's so depressed; I hope he doesn't do**
30 **anything desperate! I'm going to have to be so careful with**
31 **this power God has given me over the opposite sex.** *(To*
32 *SCOTT)* **It was fun, Scott. I'll never forget you. Bye!** *(BOTH*
33 *walk off opposite sides of stage and look back at each other making*
34 *joyous jestures of relief.)*
35

45

UP IN SMOKE

1 *CAST:* Doug and Bill
2 *AT RISE:* Bill is holding a cigarette, and Doug is handing him an
3 ashtray.
4
5 **DOUG: Bill, put out that disgusting cigarette. You're polluting**
6 **your lungs and mine.**
7 **BILL: I'm a big boy, and it's my body. I like to smoke. My dad**
8 **smokes, my brothers smoke, my grandma and aunts all**
9 **smoked.**
10 **DOUG: I noticed some of those were in the past tense. How**
11 **many of them are alive to tell about it?**
12 **BILL: Well, Uncle Henry and Uncle Jim died of heart attacks.**
13 **The doctors said smoking *might* have been a contributing**
14 **factor.**
15 **DOUG: Any other casualties?**
16 **BILL: Well, Granddad and his two brothers both ended up**
17 **with emphysema . . . had to use oxygen tanks at night to**
18 **breathe. Nobody in the house could sleep because of their**
19 **coughing. Dad's that way now. Mom makes him sleep in**
20 **the back bedroom.**
21 **DOUG: And you still smoke?**
22 **BILL: I don't have a problem. I can smoke two packs a day**
23 **and it doesn't bother me a bit.**
24 **DOUG: Didn't you have to get out of class yesterday with a**
25 **coughing jag?**
26 **BILL: Oh, that. I just . . . ah . . . choked. Yeah, I choked. Some**
27 **of Mr. Kolb's lectures are hard to swallow. You know that!**
28 **DOUG: You know, there's lots of help out there — hypnosis,**
29 **the patches, acupuncture.**
30 **BILL: Yeah, I know . . . and some day, if it ever gets to me, I'll**
31 **give some of it a try.**
32 **DOUG: It's never too early to break a bad habit, Bill.**
33 **BILL: Thanks for the advice, Doug. I'll think about what you**

1 **said. Mom's on my case, too . . . and it is an expensive**
2 **habit . . . and girls hate my cigarette breath. Maybe I**
3 **should at least cut down . . . save a little dough for my**
4 **college fund. Yeah, I'll give it some thought. I could chew**
5 **gum. Yep, I'll stop after this pack. Oh, heck, I'll throw**
6 **these away.** *(Tosses pack into audience.)* **Thanks, Doug. Now**
7 **maybe Coach'll let me back on the track team if I get so**
8 **I can breathe!**
9
10
11
12
13
14
15
16
17
18
19
20
21
22
23
24
25
26
27
28
29
30
31
32
33
34
35

46

TASSELS AND TEARS

1 ***CAST:*** Jenna and Dina
2 ***AT RISE:*** The two girls (in caps and gowns) are sitting in chairs
3 facing the audience.
4
5 **JENNA: Look out there . . . what a crowd!**
6 **DINA: Yeah, everybody can't wait to see our class graduate.**
7 **JENNA: We were known as the Class From Hell!**
8 **DINA: We put several teachers in the looney bin.**
9 **JENNA: And they said we had no creativity!**
10 **DINA: Remember when we filled Ms. Kelly's desk drawer with**
11 **baby chicks?**
12 **JENNA: Remember when we spent a week cleaning the gum**
13 **from under every desk in the building?**
14 **DINA: It was worth it!**
15 **JENNA: And all those crank calls to Mr. Collins.**
16 **DINA: I almost passed out from all that heavy breathing.**
17 **JENNA: Thank heavens we're more mature now.**
18 **DINA: Jenna, you put glue on the Valedictorian's chair!**
19 **JENNA: Well, she was too smug about being the smartest girl**
20 **in the class.**
21 **DINA: Yeah, I don't think she won it fair and square. I saw**
22 **her bringing homemade candy to the selection team.**
23 **JENNA: Guess we could have done that.**
24 **DINA: Remember, we both made Ds in Home Ec.**
25 **JENNA: Right. But she also did a king-size job of kissing up**
26 **to the teachers. We could have done that.**
27 **DINA: *Us?* We never had a chance. We were always put in**
28 **the back row where we needed binoculars to see the**
29 **teacher.**
30 **JENNA: Maybe that's why we got into so much trouble and**
31 **didn't make good grades . . . we couldn't hear the lectures.**
32 **DINA: We couldn't hear because we always had Walkmans**
33 **on our ears!**

1 **JENNA: That, too! Well, I'll have revenge when our dear,**
2 **sweet Valedictorian tears the backside out of her gown**
3 **when she gets up to deliver her speech!**
4 **DINA: Look, there's your folks. Is that your rich Grandma?**
5 **JENNA: Yep, Granny's taking me car shopping tomorrow.**
6 **DINA: Lucky you. I got a set of luggage.**
7 **JENNA: Where are your folks?**
8 **DINA: Dad's in the front row with the video camera. He's**
9 **recorded every phase of my life from the losing of the first**
10 **tooth. Mom's over to the side with boyfriend number six**
11 **hundred and forty-seven.**
12 **JENNA: I'll sure be glad when this day's over.**
13 **DINA: Me, too. Mom's throwing a little party for me, and I**
14 **invited Dad. I know there will be fireworks. They'll forget**
15 **all about my graduation they'll be so busy arguing about**
16 **who's going to pay for my college fees.**
17 **JENNA: Are you for sure going to college?**
18 **DINA: I'll do anything to get away from this scene. Besides,**
19 **I want to be a nurse . . . make people feel better. What are**
20 **your plans?**
21 **JENNA: Granny will send me any place I want to go. I'd really**
22 **like to go to UCLA and become an actress. Watch out,**
23 **Whoopie!**
24 **DINA: That's great. You always got the lead in all the plays,**
25 **and you're always "on-stage."**
26 **JENNA: I certainly am now, but I'm not getting enough**
27 **limelight. I don't like sharing the attention with this whole**
28 **class.**
29 **DINA: It'll soon be over — our high school years, our**
30 **adolescence. I think I'm beginning to feel a tear.**
31 **JENNA: What, you . . . Ms. Hardheart who couldn't wait to**
32 **split this scene . . . feeling melancholy?**
33 **DINA: I can't believe it myself, but there's something about**
34 **knowing it's the last time we'll be with this class from**
35 **hell . . . knowing we'll never gripe about cafeteria food**

1 **again, never be left off the honor roll, never make**
2 **cheerleader or drill team . . .**
3 **JENNA: Stop it, you're going to make me cry!**
4 **DINA: Well, the music is starting. Our high school days are**
5 **no more. Congratulations, Jenna.**
6 **JENNA: Congratulations, graduate. Let's sniff up our tears**
7 **and get this show on the road!** *(Both sniff.)*
8
9
10
11
12
13
14
15
16
17
18
19
20
21
22
23
24
25
26
27
28
29
30
31
32
33
34
35

Skits

47

CHORUS SLIME

1 *CAST:* Mitch, Steve and Kelly
2 *SETTING:* Three chairs are facing the audience, and a make-up
3 table is On-stage loaded with cosmetics.
4 *AT RISE:* The three players, dressed in colorful, full skirts and
5 dark pantyhose, are applying make-up to their masculine faces
6 as the curtain opens.
7
8 MITCH: *(Pulling his pantyhose over muscular legs)* **I can't do it.**
9 **These legs were made to wear knee pads, football pants,**
10 **boxer shorts . . . but *never* peek-a-boo pantyhose.**
11 KELLY: **Quit the whining, Mitch. Your mommy's not here to**
12 **give you a Tootsie Pop and make it all better.**
13 STEVE: **Whoever came up with the idea of senior jocks doing**
14 **the chorus line for the graduation assembly?**
15 KELLY: **It's tradition. My dad did it and he's as old as dirt.**
16 MITCH: **If I'd known I'd be forced to put eye shadow on, I**
17 **would have played Ping-Pong instead of football.**
18 STEVE: **Coach said that's what you *were* playing, Mitch.**
19 MITCH: **Look who's talking. You look better in a Cross Your**
20 **Heart than you ever did in a football jersey.**
21 STEVE: *(Sticking his "stuffed" shirt out)* **Oh, yeah? Well, at least**
22 **my buns don't look like two lopsided Hefty bags.**
23 MITCH: **No, your buns look like Aunt Jemima rejects.**
24 KELLY: **Ladies, ladies . . . insults won't help. When the music**
25 **plays, we have to strut these cutesy bods out on that stage**
26 **and shake, rattle and roll.**
27 STEVE: **Not easy to do when our feet are crammed into female**
28 **footwear . . . three sizes too small.**
29 MITCH: **They don't make women's shoes the size of canoes,**
30 **Steve.**
31 STEVE: **Yeah, and they don't make make-up thick enough to**
32 **hide that ugly mug of yours.** *(Looks at MITCH's face.)* **You**
33 **didn't even shave, man. You'll never be a cover girl!**

1 MITCH: You're just jealous because you've never had to put
2 a blade in your razor!
3 KELLY: Knock it off, you two. Now get your faces on. The
4 music will begin any minute. I sure hate for Tonya to see
5 me looking like this. It could damage the relationship.
6 STEVE: I doubt it. You look just like her old lady . . . except
7 you've got better looking legs.
8 MITCH: And *you* don't have a mustache.
9 STEVE: I'm the one who should be worried. I don't have a
10 date yet for the graduation dance and no self-respecting
11 girl will go with me after I've been seen in public with
12 bosoms.
13 MITCH: No self-respecting girl has *ever* gone with you!
14 STEVE: I don't see girls throwing themselves at you, Romeo
15 Breath!
16 MITCH: I've had my share of women.
17 STEVE: In your dreams, man. You haven't had a date since
18 the hula hoop!
19 MITCH: Well, at least I don't have to sit by my grandma at
20 R-rated movies.
21 STEVE: Hey, I'm just explaining the smutty words to her.
22 KELLY: Steve, you've flunked every vocabulary test since
23 preschool.
24 MITCH: Yeah, he's the only one who gets his four-letter words
25 confused when he's writing on bathroom walls.
26 STEVE: I'm going to show you jerks how good my vocab is
27 if you don't both shut up and let me put on my lip gloss.
28 *(Works on his mouth.)*
29 KELLY: I prefer letting Tonya apply my lip gloss . . . directly
30 from her lips to mine.
31 MITCH: Doesn't that pass a lot of germs?
32 KELLY: Maybe, but it's worth it. You should try it, Mitch.
33 STEVE: Only somebody doing a science experiment would
34 lock lips with Mitch.
35 MITCH: Just like you'll have to go to the city pound to find

1 **a date for the graduation dance, Steve.**
2 **KELLY: Now, girls, it's not ladylike to be witchy to our fellow**
3 **dancers. Here, have a little blush!** *(Dabs some blush on both*
4 *faces.)*
5 **MITCH: I don't want to go out there looking like this. I was**
6 **an Eagle Scout!**
7 **STEVE: I'm going to be a Marine!** *(Sings Marine Hymn.)*
8 **MITCH: Don't count on it! They're not looking for a few good**
9 **men . . . in frilly undies.**
10 **KELLY: I look so dorky they'll probably take away my**
11 **valedictorian plaque. I'll be enrolled in college classes with**
12 **kids who still have to use rounded scissors.**
13 **STEVE: You do look like something my garbage disposal spit**
14 **up.**
15 **MITCH: Don't worry, Kelly, you were voted the senior most**
16 **likely to buy out Donald Trump.**
17 **KELLY: That's right. Bet that rich dude never painted his lips**
18 **and twisted his tush in public. I'm ruined.**
19 **STEVE: Yep, after tonight you'll be on the same social**
20 **standing as Mitch and myself.**
21 **MITCH: Right. You'll be copying down phone numbers from**
22 **public walls just to hear a friendly voice.**
23 **STEVE: The only kisses you receive will be big, wet**
24 **ones . . . from your granny and dog.**
25 **KELLY: I'll be calling *The National Enquirer* with an Elvis**
26 **sighting.** *(Music heard in background.)*
27 **MITCH: Listen, I hear the music playing. We're going on in**
28 **minutes.**
29 **STEVE: OK, troops . . . attention! Shoulders back, chest out.**
30 *(They stand sideways, exposing "manly" chests to the audience.)*
31 **Man your wigs.** *(All plop on a wig.)* **We're ready for the**
32 **attack.**
33 **KELLY: I don't want to go to battle . . . I'm going AWOL!**
34 **MITCH: Oh, swallow your pride, Kelly. Remember, we owe**
35 **it to Coach Chebultz. He has a heart of gold.**

1 **STEVE: And a brain of one hundred percent mush to expect**
2 **us to sissify ourselves to music.**
3 **MITCH: We'll look back on this at our twenty-fifth reunion**
4 **and laugh.**
5 **STEVE: Easy for you to say. Your grandma's not standing**
6 **out there in a leather mini skirt with a video camera.**
7 **KELLY: And my Tonya will never warm up to me again. She'll**
8 **be jealous because I fill out a sweater better than she does.**
9 **MITCH: I just wish my pantyhose would quit pulling my leg**
10 **hairs.**
11 **STEVE: Leg hairs? *Leg hairs?* You didn't shave your legs?**
12 *(Grabs MITCH by the throat.)* ***You didn't shave your legs?***
13 **You said we *had* to shave our legs!**
14 **MITCH:** *(Choking)* **I was kidding.**
15 **STEVE:** *(Beating his head on the floor)* **You were kidding. I can't**
16 **go to the beach all summer because of stubble legs and**
17 ***you were kidding.* I knicked my legs fourteen times, lost**
18 **three pints of blood, had to apply a tourniquet above the**
19 **knee and *you* were kidding!** *(From Off-stage a voice says,*
20 *"And now, for your entertainment, the graduating class presents*
21 *its finest chorus line.")*
22 **KELLY: Get up, girls. What's done is done.** *(His friends get up*
23 *and straighten their clothes, primping a little.)*
24 **STEVE: So much for that deodorant that's strong enough for**
25 **a man.** *(Holds up his armpit to expose* big *wet spots.)*
26 **KELLY: Well, here goes nothing.** *(Music gets louder. The three*
27 *line up and start Off-stage doing the cancan.)*
28 **STEVE: You get in front of me, Mitch, in case my foot slips**
29 **in the cancan I want it to hit your bun-buns.**
30 **MITCH: Don't hold a grudge, Steve. It makes a big, ugly crease**
31 **in your cutesy-wootsy face.**
32 **STEVE: I'm going to knock your cutesy-wootsy teeth down**
33 **your bigsy-wigsy flappin' lips!**
34 **KELLY: Kick, girls. Yesterday we were ordinary guys,**
35 **tomorrow we'll be know-it-all high school graduates, but**

1 **tonight we're hip shakin', leg kickin', dancin' dollies!**
2 **MITCH: Oh, no . . .**
3 **STEVE: What's wrong?**
4 **MITCH: I think my Living Bra just died!**
5 **STEVE: We'll have a double funeral for it and *you* later. Now**
6 ***boogie.*** *(They cancan their way off the stage with style and*
7 *grace.)*
8
9
10
11
12
13
14
15
16
17
18
19
20
21
22
23
24
25
26
27
28
29
30
31
32
33
34
35

48

HOW TO DUMP A DIP

1 *CAST:* Pam, Kari and Kate
2 *SETTING:* Local drug store
3 *AT RISE:* The three are sitting at a table sipping sodas.
4
5 **PAM: I'm really getting bored with my life. There's no**
6 **excitement anymore.**
7 **KARI: Seventeen is too young to be bored. I feel the same way.**
8 **KATE: I think we're all in a rut.**
9 **PAM: Yeah, same school, same classes, same clubs, same**
10 **clothes and same boyfriends!**
11 **KARI: What are you saying . . . that we should change guys?**
12 **KATE: You think we should dump our steady boyfriends after**
13 **we worked so hard to get them?**
14 **KARI: We went through hell to get those guys away from their**
15 **old girlfriends . . . spread rumors, told big white lies, set**
16 **up accidental meetings.**
17 **KATE: It was the biggest campaign of our lives. I filled a**
18 **whole diary with our little underhanded tricks. Now you**
19 **say we should terminate the relationships just so we won't**
20 **be bored?**
21 **PAM: Were we bored while we were plotting little schemes**
22 **to entrap the guys?**
23 **KARI: No, it was the most exciting time of my life.**
24 **KATE: I couldn't sleep because my little brain was cooking**
25 **up other ways to snare the men of our dreams.**
26 **PAM: Do you still feel the same way about them?**
27 **KARI: No, they are far from perfect, but what if we can't**
28 **replace them?**
29 **KATE: And prom is coming up in a couple of months.**
30 **PAM: That will make it more of a challenge. We'll have to**
31 **think of creative ways to dump these guys and get**
32 **replacements before the prom.**
33 **KATE: I don't want to take a chance on going stag to the**

1 **biggest event of the year.**
2 **PAM: You can always go with Richard. He's followed you**
3 **around like a little puppy dog since third grade.**
4 **KATE: My little brother's best friend with a crush doesn't**
5 **appeal to me as the ideal prom date.**
6 **KARI: Steve is no Mel Gibson, but I'm afraid to dump him**
7 **without a substitute standing by.**
8 **PAM: We snagged those three without any problems. We'll**
9 **begin plotting our strategies as soon as we lose our excess**
10 **baggage. So the biggest problem we have now is how to**
11 **dump these fellows without everybody thinking we're**
12 **super witches.**
13 **KATE: If it gets out that we trick guys into going steady with**
14 **us just so we can dump them later, our reputations will**
15 **be ruined.**
16 **KARI: Yeah, you know how guys talk!**
17 **PAM: Well, the trick is to dump them in such a way they think**
18 **they wanted to break up with us.**
19 **KARI: I think Steve is ready to call it quits. He's been bringing**
20 **a book along on our dates.**
21 **KATE: I don't think Kip will be too heartbroken either. He**
22 **chose to stay home and mow the lawn instead of going to**
23 **the ballgame with me . . . and it was his favorite team**
24 **playing!**
25 **PAM: See, we'll look on it as an act of mercy . . . cutting the**
26 **ties that bind these guys to us.**
27 **KATE: Yeah, with a real sharp knife!**
28 **KARI: Like tearing off a Band-Aid: one quick rip!**
29 **PAM: Now the question is: *How* do we do it?**
30 **KATE: Well, there is that song about so many ways to leave**
31 **your lover.**
32 **KARI: We'll need to be more creative than that. I could tell**
33 **Steve I have an incurable disease . . . and contagious!**
34 **PAM: That would sure make other guys trip over each other**
35 **trying to date you.**

1 KARI: Oh, right.
2 KATE: Well, I think I'll just take the direct route . . . set Kip
3 down, rip off his headphones, and tell him it's over . . .
4 David Copperfield couldn't restore the magic.
5 PAM: Good plan, and with Kip it'll work. You may have to
6 spell it out for him in three-letter words, but I think it'll
7 work. Now, how do you leave Steve?
8 KARI: The direct route won't work with him. I guess I'll have
9 to tell his little sister. She really likes me and thinks I'm
10 too good for Steve. She'd be thrilled to drop the bomb on
11 him, and she's good with weapons! Yes, I'll go talk to Polly
12 and let her do my dirty work.
13 KATE: Sounds like it'll do the job. Now, Pam, how are you
14 going to dump Mr. Wonderful?
15 PAM: It'll be a little tricky, but I've got it all worked out. I've
16 already sent him three notes from Tara saying how she's
17 dying to go out with him *if* he'd just get rid of me! I noticed
18 he had her name written on his notebook yesterday. He
19 spelled it wrong, of course, but nobody goes with Rock
20 for his brains! So he'll drool in gratitude when I tell him
21 he's just too good for me.
22 KARI: Great scheme. I guess we're all on our way to
23 widowhood.
24 KATE: Yeah, wish we'd had some kind of insurance policy
25 on them!
26 PAM: But there are fringe benefits.
27 KARI: Right. We can start flirting again!
28 KATE: It will be fun to check out the gym, sit behind the
29 football bench . . .
30 KARI: But let's be a little bit choosier this time.
31 PAM: Maybe we'll want to choose guys with a few more brain
32 cells. Ones that understand things other than motorcycles
33 and football plays.
34 KATE: Well, that sure narrows the field.
35 PAM: Remember, it's not long till the prom, so we'll have to

1 choose our next victims soon . . . and plot . . . and
2 rehearse . . .
3 KARI: Oh, goody. There's this new guy in my lit class . . .
4 PAM: No hitting on anybody till we've done our dumping.
5 KATE: I'm off to have my direct talk right now. Meet you
6 back here this evening.
7 KARI: I can catch Polly at her dance class. I'll buy her an ice
8 cream cone while I explain her mission.
9 PAM: I know somebody who's dying to have "Tara" tattooed
10 on his chest, so I'll just go let him off the hook.
11 KATE: Let's meet back here at seven . . . single women!
12 KARI: Free to scope the hunks.
13 PAM: Right. But now we must do our dastardly deeds. We've
14 got to go dump some dips!
15
16
17
18
19
20
21
22
23
24
25
26
27
28
29
30
31
32
33
34
35

WINGIN' IT

1 ***CAST:*** Six aspiring angels (3M, 3W) and Gabe in sheets (robes).
2 ***SETTING:*** This skit takes place in the clouds with a gate in the
3 background. Also, a phone and a large chalkboard with the
4 numbers one to six and "Aspiring Angels" written above the
5 numbers.
6 ***AT RISE:*** Gabe, the keeper of the gate, is hanging up the celestial
7 phone and placing another mark under number two.
8
9 **GABE: Another good remark for you, Number Two. Just**
10 **three more people down there on earth praising you, and**
11 **you'll slide right through the teenage section of the Pearly**
12 **Gates.**
13 **#2: I can't figure out what's taking so long. I was a model**
14 **teenager . . . Student Council president, basketball captain,**
15 **big brother to an orphan.** *(Looks down from the stage.)* **What's**
16 **wrong with you people down there?**
17 **#1: Loosen up, man. I've been in this holding tank for two**
18 **months and look at my score. Ain't nobody got any good**
19 **comments to say about me.**
20 **#4: Oh, I'm sure you're wrong, Number One. Why surely your**
21 **mother, your old aunt, your girlfriend, your homeroom**
22 **teacher . . . somebody has been missing you.**
23 **#1: Nope. My old lady kicked me out of the house when I was**
24 **thirteen. I lived in the alley most of the time. They kicked**
25 **me out of school . . . said I was a major disturbance.**
26 **#3: They said that about me, too. I was the class clown. Count**
27 **on me to put a whoopie cushion under the English**
28 **teacher's buns . . . put frogs in all the stools in the girls'**
29 **restrooms. Those were the days! But look at my score. I**
30 **only need three more votes and I get to crash the big gate.**
31 **#5: I don't want to go through the gate. I don't want to be**
32 **here. I want to wake up and find this is a horrible dream.**
33 **I want to be in my room with my cat Fluffy curled up at**

1 my feet. *(Sniffs.)*
2 #2: **Well, it's too late. We've all crossed over. We can't go home**
3 **again. The best thing to hope for is that we'll get twenty-**
4 **five kind comments about us from down there. If we are**
5 **missed, I guess that means we lived a good enough life . . .**
6 **that we were loved and deserve to go through those big**
7 **toll gates in the sky.**
8 #1: **Bummer. That's too much to pay. Another of life's rip-offs.**
9 *(Phone rings. GABE answers, shakes his head. The six would-be*
10 *ANGELS look down off the front of the stage to see if they can*
11 *see anybody they know and watch anxiously as GABE gets the*
12 *chalk, looks from person to person, and chalks another mark for*
13 *#3.)*
14 #3: **'Atta girl, Ms. Klenky. She was my drama coach. I made**
15 **her hair turn prematurely grey. I was her reason for**
16 **signing up for weekly sessions at a shrink, and I take**
17 **credit for getting her headed down the menopausal road.**
18 #4: **If you were that horrid to her, why would she make a**
19 **kind comment about you?**
20 #3: **I was always teacher's pet! Even if I drove them nuts, they**
21 **couldn't help but love me. I made them laugh! You know,**
22 **teachers need all the laughs they can get.**
23 #1: **Most teachers *are* a laugh. What's your story, Number Six?**
24 #6: **Story? I don't have a "story." This whole thing is a mistake.**
25 **I don't belong here with the rest of you. I'm a Clairmont . . .**
26 **of the Clairmont Bank, Clairmont Department Store . . . of**
27 **the city of Clairmont!**
28 #2: **Here there are no names . . . you're just Number Six.**
29 #6: **I won't stand for this. I know Daddy has made**
30 **arrangements for me to get through the first-class gate.**
31 **You there, Mr. Gatekeeper. There's a big tip in it for you**
32 **if you'll let me use your phone. I need to call Daddy.**
33 GABE: **Sorry, Number Six. This phone only works one way.**
34 **It only rings when somebody down there has a kind word**
35 **to say about one of you wing seekers. No out-going calls.**

1 #6: You've got to be kidding. What kind of a place is this? I
2 demand to see your supervisor.
3 GABE: I'm afraid my boss is engaged in other activities. He
4 doesn't get involved with new recruits till they fill their
5 scorecard. *(Phone rings.)* Excuse me. *(Listens, nods his head*
6 *and makes three marks for #5.)*
7 #3: Congratulations! Triple play. That's some kind of record,
8 Number Five.
9 #5: I don't want marks. I need to go home. My mother can't
10 make it without me. She's in a wheelchair and completely
11 dependent upon me. There's nobody to help her.
12 #1: Calm down. It's a tough place down there. I don't know
13 why anybody would ever want to go back. I'm much
14 happier here than I ever was down there.
15 #6: Well I'm not staying here. When my dad turns his lawyers
16 loose, you'll all see what a Clairmont can do. Now, tell me
17 how to get out of here.
18 GABE: Sorry, but each of you is here by invitation.
19 #3: An invitation too good to turn down, right?
20 #1: What we got were one-way tickets.
21 #6: I always travel charter.
22 #2: Not this trip, Number Six. You're just a number like the
23 rest of us.
24 #6: I beg your pardon. I'm *not* like the rest of you!
25 #3: Right. She doesn't have as many marks as we do!
26 #6: I don't get this mark business. I'm sure my father can buy
27 me anything I'll need. Or the money could be transferred
28 from my trust fund. Mr. Gabe, let me talk to the person in
29 charge of finances.
30 GABE: There is no currency here. The rewards come from
31 below when someone remembers you . . . misses you . . .
32 sings your praises.
33 #6: My dad could hire the Metropolitan Opera to sing for me.
34 I just need to get him the message. He wears a beeper.
35 #1: You just don't get it, rich girl. Your Visa's canceled, your

1 Swiss bank accounts are closed, your rich daddy can't
2 bail you out anymore.
3 #2: He's right. We're all on our own. We're too young to be
4 facing this. We didn't understand. We weren't prepared.
5 #4: And we thought we had lots of years to figure out life's
6 mysteries.
7 #3: We thought we were invincible. I'll never get to be on
8 Letterman or publish my joke book.
9 #4: I'll never be a doctor . . . or a mother.
10 #1: I'll never be in another jail cell or go hungry again.
11 #2: I won't get to finish law school and run for senator.
12 #3: Good thing. Gabe would never be charting you any marks
13 if you were in Congress!
14 #5: I really need to check on my mother.
15 #2: Can you see her down there? *(All look Off-stage.)* I see my
16 brother . . . driving my convertible!
17 #3: I see my mom reading the pages of my joke book, and
18 she's smiling. That's the first time she's smiled in weeks!
19 I'm glad I wrote all those funny lines. Mom looks like she
20 needs a laugh.
21 #1: I see my parole officer making some other kid's life
22 miserable.
23 #4: I see my sister trying on my clothes. We were twins, you
24 know.
25 #6: There's Daddy! *Daddy*, up here. I really need you. He's
26 getting into the limo, driving away. I don't know what to
27 do. I've never been on my own before . . . alone and
28 forgotten.
29 #4: We're all here together. Nobody's alone.
30 #2: And the marks show that we're not forgotten.
31 #5: I don't see my mother. There's her wheelchair, but it's
32 empty! *(Phone rings. GABE answers, marks #5.)*
33 GABE: Looks like Number Five made the quota. The gates
34 are opening.
35 #5: No, I can't go. I need to go back below . . . check on Mama.

1 **GABE: It will be OK, Number Five. Just grab your wings and**
2 **cross over.**
3 **#3: Look on the other side of the gate. There's a lady waving**
4 **at you, Number Five.**
5 **#5: What? Why, it's . . . Mama. It's Mama. She's already there.**
6 **Mama, you're walking . . . and smiling. I'm coming, Mama.**
7 *(Exits through the gates.)*
8 **#2: Well, all's well that ends well, I guess.**
9 **#1: I'm glad Number Five had a happy ending.** *(Phone rings.*
10 *GABE keeps nodding, nodding, goes to board and puts twenty-*
11 *five marks for #1.)*
12 **#1: What?! There's gotta be a technical error. I don't even**
13 **know twenty-five people.** *(Looks down at audience.)* **Oh, it's**
14 **that Boy Scout troop that was lost in the woods. It was**
15 **nothing. I knew that forest better than anybody. It was**
16 **my home in the summer! Well, who would have thought**
17 **it . . . son-of-a-gun . . . oops, is that a bad phrase?**
18 **GABE: It's permissible. Grab your wings, Number One, and**
19 **pass through.**
20 **#1: Take heart, gang, don't give up. You'll all make it through.**
21 **If a guy like me can get through these pearly gates, there's**
22 **hope for everyone.** *(Grabs wings, touches them tenderly,*
23 *salutes the others.)* **Well, son-of-a-gun!** *(Walks through the gates*
24 *as others wave.)*
25
26
27
28
29
30
31
32
33
34
35

50

A FEW GOOD MEN

1 *CAST:* Troy, Robert, Kent and Brian.
2 *SETTING:* Four guys are sitting at a table, sipping pop from
3 bottles.
4 *AT RISE:* Robert stands up and tries on his graduation cap. Others
5 continue sipping and watching.
6
7 **ROBERT: Well, in another week we'll all be high school**
8 **graduates.**
9 **TROY: Well, maybe not *all*.** *(All look at BRIAN.)*
10 **BRIAN: Hey, I'm getting my term paper in. With my superior**
11 **intellect it takes longer to compose great manuscripts.**
12 **KENT: The kind of manuscripts your brain produces has**
13 **lined many bird cages!**
14 **ROBERT: Yeah, the paper was due three weeks ago.**
15 **BRIAN: I had to meditate.**
16 **KENT: You're gonna vegetate . . . right here at old** *(Your high*
17 *school)* **High while the rest of us go on to college.**
18 **TROY: Or the Marines! Remember how we took a blood oath**
19 **to join when we were eighteen?**
20 **ROBERT: We were only seven when we took that sacred oath.**
21 **KENT: And it was written in Kool-Aid, not blood!**
22 **TROY: Doesn't matter. We made a pact . . . a solemn vow . . . to**
23 **be a few of the strong, the brave, the chosen.** *(Others hum*
24 *a patriotic song as TROY puts his hand across his heart and*
25 *delivers this line.)*
26 **ROBERT: I don't think I'm ready to be that tough.**
27 **TROY: Sure we are. Didn't Coach say we were the strongest**
28 **ones on the team?**
29 **KENT: I think he was talking about our breath, Troy.**
30 **BRIAN: I couldn't join the corp, anyway. My mama wouldn't**
31 **let me!**
32 **ALL: Baby. Mama's Boy. Him's mommy won't let him!**
33 **BRIAN: Well, it's true. And I can't see you guys giving up**

1 your freedom to protect your country either.
2 KENT: It might be worth it . . . no more classes, no more
3 school lunch or homework.
4 ROBERT: Since when did you ever do homework?
5 KENT: Never. But it was quite a strain thinking up all those
6 creative excuses.
7 TROY: You will go down in the *Guinness*, Kent, for most
8 excuses offered . . . and not believed!
9 KENT: I guess my image would take quite a boost if I became
10 a Marine.
11 TROY: Right! We'd be heroes. Parades would be thrown in
12 our honor. We'd have our manly chests plastered with
13 purple medals.
14 BRIAN: We'll have to develop chests first!
15 TROY: We will. We'll be up at five . . . climb fences and ropes,
16 crawl for miles on our stomachs, eat canned meat in fox
17 holes, listen for enemy fire . . .
18 KENT: I think you've been watching too many old John
19 Wayne movies, Troy.
20 ROBERT: You haven't mentioned the best reason to become
21 a Marine.
22 ALL: *Women!*
23 ROBERT: Right. They can't resist a man in uniform.
24 BRIAN: I'm not so sure. I wore a uniform once and it didn't
25 help a bit.
26 KENT: A Chicken Joe's hat and feathered apron doesn't cut
27 it, Brian!
28 TROY: But if we walked down Main Street in our Marine
29 gear, girls would drop at our feet. We could have our pick
30 of the litter.
31 KENT: We've dated enough dogs, Troy.
32 ROBERT: If you guys could guarantee me that females would
33 be crawling all over this lush body *and* that I wouldn't get
34 hurt, I'd sign today.
35 TROY: Nobody can promise, Robert, but what do you have

1 to lose?
2 **ROBERT:** My freedom, my butt . . .
3 **BRIAN:** I guess I could be a Marine. I just wouldn't tell
4 Mommy . . . just leave her a note on my pillow.
5 **KENT:** It does sound better than college, where I'd have to
6 continue making up all those excuses for not doing my
7 assignments. I was looking forward to sorority girls
8 though!
9 **ROBERT:** We can still have sorority girls. They'll prefer us
10 in our rugged combat boots to nerdy frat boys.
11 **BRIAN:** I'll go finish my term paper. I don't want to be stuck
12 with latrine duty because I don't have my diploma. I'd
13 better start my letter to Mommy, too. See ya soon, fellow
14 servicemen! *(Leaves.)*
15 **TROY:** I'm not *real* sure Brian's Marine material.
16 **KENT:** Sure. He's just what they're looking for . . . someone
17 who'll show a *lot* of progress!
18 **ROBERT:** Right. If they can't make a man out of Brian,
19 nobody can.
20 **KENT:** But they're just looking for a *few* of us.
21 **TROY:** Just hope Brian's old lady won't be bunking with us
22 in our barracks.
23 **KENT:** Don't think Mommy can pass the physical.
24 **TROY:** Well, men, we've taken the first step. We're going to
25 be winners, not wimps!
26 **ROBERT:** We're going to make a name for ourselves.
27 **KENT:** Watch out blood and guts!
28 **TROY:** This is great. We're all going to be all that we can
29 be — Marines. *(All march out singing "From the Halls of*
30 *Montezuma.")*
31
32
33
34
35

51

SISTER ACT

CAST: Lisa, 16-year-old teenager; Nikki, older sister; Lindsay, younger sister; Carrie, Lisa's friend; Mother.

SETTING: The scene is in a typical teenager's bedroom — in disarray.

AT RISE: Lisa is leisurely lying on the bed reading as Lindsay enters.

LISA: Don't you know to knock before you barge into someone's room? I could have been having a private conversation or dressing.

LINDSAY: Or cleaning your room? Ha! This place is a mess. Mom's gonna have a cow. She has bridge club tonight and we're supposed to have our rooms spotless so her snooty friends won't trip on any cobwebs.

LISA: Nobody should stick her nose in my room.

LINDSAY: Well, they will. One of those phoney females will pretend she needs to potty and got the wrong door, just so she can see if the wallpaper and the curtains match. All of Mom's friends are such snoops! *(NIKKI enters.)*

LISA: Speaking of snoops, here's our dearly loved big sister.

NIKKI: Don't try to kiss up. Which one of you family rejects stole my diary?

LISA: Why would we want to steal anything as dull as your diary?

NIKKI: Dull? You think my life is dull? Neither of you will ever have the long list of boyfriends, the social standing, the popularity I have! All of the good genes from both sides of the family came to me. You were both served leftovers.

LINDSAY: But when the family brains were dished out, Nikki just got table scraps! And how do you know somebody stole your diary. It's probably on your make-up table . . . covered with all that stuff you glob on your face. Or under

1 a ton of that junk jewelry you wear.
2 LISA: Right. Snoopy almost choked to death on one of your
3 snail earrings you left on the floor.
4 LINDSAY: Yeah. I had to give him CPR.
5 NIKKI: Did you save the earring?
6 LINDSAY: Nope. But I pumped up a shoestring, a hairball
7 and part of Dad's missing purple sock.
8 NIKKI: What was that mutt doing in my room anyway? And
9 what were you two doing in there?
10 LISA: We were on a junk food pilgrimage.
11 NIKKI: You know I've been watching my weight, eating only
12 carrot sticks and yogurt.
13 LISA: Ha! Yesterday I saw you at the Dairy Queen with Eric
14 Powers eating a banana split.
15 NIKKI: That doesn't count. It was business. I was lining up
16 a date for the prom.
17 LINDSAY: Does your digestive tract and your butt know
18 those calories don't count?
19 LISA: Besides, Snoopy and I found Milk Duds, Doritos and
20 Oreos in your pantyhose drawer.
21 NIKKI: You little maggots. Mom and Dad should have
22 practiced better birth control after they had me. And if I
23 find that either of you had my diary, I *will* be an only child!
24 *(Exits.)*
25 LINDSAY: Why do you think she acts like that?
26 LISA: Has something to do with her hormones.
27 LINDSAY: She'll outgrow it?
28 LISA: Well, I'm not sure; Aunt Shirley's always acted just like
29 that and she's pushin' fifty!
30 LINDSAY: I'd say Nikki just inherited an overdose of the
31 Sanders' "Twinkieville" traits. Thank goodness we took
32 after Mom's side of the family.
33 LISA: Right. Do you have Nikki's diary?
34 LINDSAY: No. I tried to read it, but all those misspelled
35 words, cheese dip dribbles on the pages and tall tales . . . if

1 I want to read science fiction, I'll turn to Stephen King.
2 LISA: So what did you do with the diary?
3 LINDSAY: I put it in a safe place . . . a place she'll never think
4 to look.
5 LISA: On her bookshelf with her unused textbooks?
6 LINDSAY: Nope. Took the cover off the new Bible Grandma
7 gave her and wrapped it around the diary. Maybe it'll
8 purify some of the stuff she wrote in there!
9 LISA: Good move. You're really growing up to be a clever
10 girl, Lindsay.
11 LINDSAY: Thanks, it's an art! *(CARRIE enters.)* Oh, no, it's
12 your goofy friend, Carrie.
13 CARRIE: Hello, squirt. When are you going to grow
14 up . . . start wearing Cross Your Hearts and deodorant?
15 LINDSAY: When are you going to get a personality of your
16 own? I imagine Miss Piggy would like to have hers back.
17 Well, I'd love to hang around and hear your stimulating
18 conversation, Carrie . . . all the boys who aren't good
19 enough for you . . . all the boys who are dying to spread
20 their coats across mud puddles for you . . . all the boys
21 who will commit suicide if you don't smile in their
22 direction. Mother Goose could have used some of those
23 plots. *(Exits.)*
24 CARRIE: There must have been a mix-up at the hospital. I
25 can't believe you branched from the same family tree as
26 those two sisters of yours.
27 LISA: Yep, it's hard to believe. We're all so different.
28 CARRIE: Thank heavens for that. I wouldn't be caught dead
29 running around with anyone like Nikki or Lindsay!
30 LISA: Oh, sometimes they're not so bad. What's on our agenda
31 today?
32 CARRIE: I thought we'd head for the mall. They're having a
33 big sale on guys' tank tops.
34 LISA: Why do we want to look at tank tops?
35 CARRIE: *Think!* It's not the tank tops . . . it's what's going to

1 be *in* the tank tops!
2 LISA: Oh . . .
3 BOTH: *Hunks!*
4 LISA: How do you think of all these things, Carrie? It would
5 never occur to me to look at the sale ads for guys.
6 CARRIE: That's why you have me for a friend. Let's head for
7 the mall.
8 LISA: I'm really supposed to clean my room. Mom's having
9 bridge club tonight.
10 CARRIE: So?
11 LISA: Bridge clubbers seem to think they have search
12 warrants to poke their curious noses into any room they
13 want.
14 CARRIE: Well, we'll be back in plenty of time to clean this
15 mess up. We just want to watch the guys strut and flex in
16 those tank tops.
17 LISA: It sounds a little like window peeking to me.
18 CARRIE: Right, but it's not illegal! *(MOTHER enters.)*
19 MOTHER: What's not illegal?
20 CARRIE: Hot fudge sundaes. They're fattening, but not
21 illegal.
22 MOTHER: This room is illegal, Lisa. Now start cleaning it up,
23 then I'll need a little help downstairs.
24 LISA: What's wrong with Nikki?
25 MOTHER: I don't have time to go into that. No, Nikki is
26 scrubbing the kitchen floor as we speak.
27 LISA: Nikki . . . on her knees!
28 MOTHER: Now, Lisa, Nikki has her good points. By the way,
29 do you know what happened to her diary? She's really
30 upset.
31 LISA: I'm sure she'll find it, and her being on her knees is a
32 good start.
33 MOTHER: What?
34 LISA: Nothing. Sorry, Carrie, I can't go to the mall. Mommy
35 Dearest is making me clean the chimney.

1 **CARRIE: Well, I'll report back to you tonight. See ya!** *(Exits.)*
2 **MOTHER: Well, let's get this done . . . clean bedding, do these**
3 **windows. How long has it been since you've seen the top**
4 **of this desk?**
5 **LISA: Why do we have to work just because you want to have**
6 **a party? It isn't fair.**
7 **MOTHER: Is it fair that I have to clean, bake cakes, fix pizza,**
8 **get prizes, haul kids home, etc., every time one of you girls**
9 **decides to have a birthday party?**
10 **LISA: That's different . . . you're the mom.**
11 **MOTHER: And why do you think I had three girls? So I could**
12 **have cheap labor . . . now get to work!** *(Exits laughing.)*
13 **LISA: I know Nikki and Lindsay aren't having to work as**
14 **hard as I do. Nikki's Dad's pet and little Lindsay can do**
15 **no wrong in Mom's eyes. It's always the middle child that**
16 **carries the burden, gets picked on, isn't loved. I'm only**
17 **going to have** ***two*** **children — boys!**
18
19
20
21
22
23
24
25
26
27
28
29
30
31
32
33
34
35

52

DOUBLE YOUR PLEASURE

1 *CAST:* Jack, Ken, Kandi and Kookie
2 *SETTING:* At a table in a restaurant
3 *AT RISE:* Jack and Ken are drinking Cokes and talking.
4
5 **JACK: I don't know why I ever let you talk me into this double**
6 **blind date.**
7 **KEN: Look on it as an adventure.**
8 **JACK: A safari through the dangerous jungle of Africa is an**
9 **adventure, and something tells me this date will turn out**
10 **to be more hazardous to my health! I may as well smoke . . .**
11 **the Surgeon General warns against blind dating, too.**
12 **KEN: Lighten up! Look, my cousin Slate set this up for us. It**
13 **can't backfire.**
14 **JACK: Slate? Isn't he the cousin who tried to make counterfeit**
15 **money with crayons?**
16 **KEN: Yeah. Well, he learned his lesson. He's on the up and**
17 **up now. He said we'd *love* the twins.**
18 **JACK: How come he doesn't date them if they're so great?**
19 **KEN: He's tied up with Sheena, the girl doing the jungle act**
20 **at the circus.**
21 **JACK: And these two girls, our dates, are they performers,**
22 **too? Will I be able to tell my great grandchildren their**
23 **ancient grandparent once dated Flame, the sword**
24 **swallower, or Sweet Cheeks, the five-hundred-pound fat**
25 **lady?**
26 **KEN: You're so funny, Jack, and so wrong. Kandi and Kookie**
27 **don't perform at the circus.**
28 **JACK: Kookie and Kandi? I'm getting cavities just saying**
29 **their names!**
30 **KEN: Well, what do you expect? They're twins, and they do**
31 **gum commercials.**
32 **JACK: No kidding? I've seen some of those girls. They're hot!**
33 **KEN: Well, they don't do *those* commercials. They do the gum**

1 **that's more medicinal . . . laxative gum.**
2 **JACK: Of course, I should have guessed. They'll be wearing**
3 **support hose, have blue hair and be walking with canes.**
4 **KEN: No, they're blondes, and Slate said very shapely.**
5 **JACK: This is the same guy who clogged the sewer with**
6 **Bicycle cards because he wanted a royal "flush."**
7 **KEN: Hey, can I help it if high I.Q.s don't run in my family?**
8 **Look, here come the girls . . . not too bad, huh?**
9 **JACK: No, they'd look great . . . on a Vegas stage. I hope I**
10 **don't run into Grandma or any of her friends tonight. I'll**
11 **be cut out of the will! I also hope nobody on the "Who's**
12 **Who" selection board sees me, or anybody else whose**
13 **opinion I value.** *(Two rather gaudy blondes approach the table.*
14 *The boys get up.)*
15 **KEN: Hello, girls, we're glad you made it. We were getting**
16 **worried.**
17 **KANDI: We**
18 **KOOKIE: Took**
19 **KANDI: Time**
20 **KOOKIE: To**
21 **KANDI: Tone**
22 **KOOKIE: Down**
23 **KANDI: Our**
24 **KOOKIE: Wardrobe.** *(Both giggle.)*
25 **JACK: Thanks, that was thoughtful. Please sit here, out of**
26 **sight . . . I mean, out of the light!** *(Seats the girls.)*
27 **KANDI: Oh,**
28 **KOOKIE: We**
29 **KANDI: Just**
30 **KOOKIE: Knew**
31 **KANDI: You'd**
32 **KOOKIE: Be**
33 **KANDI: Gentlemen**
34 **KOOKIE: Like**
35 **KANDI: Slate!** *(They giggle.)*

1 **KEN: Manners run in the family.**
2 **JACK: Manure runs in the family!**
3 **KANDI: Oh,**
4 **KOOKIE: He's**
5 **KANDI: So**
6 **KOOKIE: Funny!** *(They giggle.)*
7 **KEN: What would you girls like to do tonight?**
8 **KANDI: We**
9 **KOOKIE: Want**
10 **KANDI: To**
11 **KOOKIE: Dance.** *(They giggle.)*
12 **KEN: Great, I know just the right place.**
13 **JACK: Across the state line, I hope!**
14 **KEN: Let's split. We've got a fun-filled evening ahead.**
15 **KANDI: Oh**
16 **KOOKIE: We**
17 **KANDI: Owe**
18 **KOOKIE: Slate**
19 **KANDI: For**
20 **KOOKIE: Setting**
21 **KANDI: Up**
22 **KOOKIE: This**
23 **KANDI: Date.** *(They giggle.)*
24 **JACK: I owe him something myself!**
25 **KEN: Come on, ladies.** *(All get up.)*
26 **KANDI: You're**
27 **KOOKIE: So**
28 **KANDI: Cute**
29 **KOOKIE: Ken.**
30 **KEN: I know, I know. Looks run in the family, too.**
31 **JACK: We're back to the manure. You three go on out to the**
32 **car. I'll take care of the tab.** *(The three start to leave.)*
33 **KANDI: Don't**
34 **KOOKIE: Take**
35 **KANDI: Too**

1 **KOOKIE: Long.**
2 **KANDI: We'll**
3 **KOOKIE: Miss**
4 **KANDI: You!** *(They giggle as three exit.)*
5 **JACK:** *(Taking money from billfold)* **I'd better take a Bufferin . . .**
6 **better make that three Bufferin.** *(Swallows the pills with his*
7 *water then looks out at the audience with both arms raised.)* **If**
8 **I live through this evening, I swear as God as my**
9 **witness . . .** *(Says this last phrase imitating the twins — back*
10 *and forth in pitched voice)* **I'll . . . never . . . go . . . on . . . a . . .**
11 **blind . . . date . . . again!** *(Exits slowly as curtain falls.)*
12
13
14
15
16
17
18
19
20
21
22
23
24
25
26
27
28
29
30
31
32
33
34
35

53

IT'S BETTER TO GIVE

1 ***CAST:*** Bart, Bruce and Phil
2 ***SETTING:*** On a city bus
3 ***AT RISE:*** The three guys have sat down, each carrying sacks.
4
5 **BART: I'm never doing that again. I hate to shop!**
6 **BRUCE: Did you ever see anything like those stores?**
7 **PHIL: People pushing and grabbing . . . and lots of them old**
8 **ladies!**
9 **BART: Shopping is women's work. Next time I'll pay my sister**
10 **to do my shopping. But she hates Alisha, so I couldn't trust**
11 **her to pick out something nice.**
12 **PHIL: What did you buy your old ball and chain?**
13 **BART: A chain with a locket on it. She can put my picture on**
14 **one side and her dog's on the other.**
15 **BRUCE: It'll be hard to tell who's who.**
16 **BART: Very funny. What did you get Chris for Valentine's**
17 **Day?**
18 **BRUCE: Something cool, something practical . . .**
19 **PHIL/BART: Something cheap!**
20 **BRUCE: A gift doesn't have to be expensive to have meaning.**
21 **I put a lot of thought into Chris' present.**
22 **BART: And hardly any money.**
23 **PHIL: How could you have put any thought into it, Bruce?**
24 **You were only gone four minutes.**
25 **BRUCE: Right. I don't agonize over little things like you guys.**
26 **PHIL: A Valentine gift isn't a little thing. Girls and flower**
27 **shops and Hallmark have made a big deal out of it!**
28 **BART: If we'd have been *real* smart, we'd have broken off**
29 **with our girlfriends last week.**
30 **PHIL: Then beg them to take us back on February 15!**
31 **BRUCE: That's not such a bad idea. *Now* you think about it**
32 **after we've wasted all this time.**
33 **PHIL: And spent big bucks.**

1 **BART: All except Bruce!**
2 **BRUCE: Hey, I'm not ashamed of my gift, but I kept the**
3 **receipt . . . if you guys want to do that dumping thing.**
4 **BART: Nah, I've already got the locket.**
5 **PHIL: And tomorrow's the fourteenth. We waited too long,**
6 **but next year . . .**
7 **BRUCE: We'll manage to have a big fight on the twentieth of**
8 **December.**
9 **PHIL: And the tenth of February.**
10 **BART: And two days before their birthdays.**
11 **BRUCE: We'll save a bundle.**
12 **PHIL: No more shopping expeditions.**
13 **BRUCE: But won't the girls catch on?**
14 **BART: Sure, after a while. We may have to switch girls along**
15 **the way.**
16 **BRUCE: But think of the money we'll save — big bucks. It'll**
17 **be worth it.**
18 **PHIL: But I'm really attracted to Kim.**
19 **BART: So?**
20 **PHIL: So I don't want to date other girls. Well, maybe Shelby.**
21 **BRUCE: And Tonya. You've been eyeballing her for weeks.**
22 **PHIL: Yeah, there's Tonya, but that doesn't mean I'm not loyal**
23 **to Kim!**
24 **BART: Well, here's our bus stop. Now, let's make a pact.**
25 **BRUCE: No more girl gifts.**
26 **PHIL: OK. We'll give these, then no more presents to females,**
27 **except our mommies and grannies.**
28 **BRUCE: Right. No more heart-shaped boxes of chocolates.**
29 **PHIL: No more cutesy stuffed animals.**
30 **BART: No more metal stuff to wear around their wrists,**
31 **fingers or necks.**
32 **BRUCE: No more allowances squandered on unappreciative**
33 **girls.**
34 **PHIL: You got it, but let's go now and deliver our final**
35 **Valentine gifts.**

1 **BART: We're men with a mission. We're playing Stupid Cupid**
2 **for the last time!**
3
4
5
6
7
8
9
10
11
12
13
14
15
16
17
18
19
20
21
22
23
24
25
26
27
28
29
30
31
32
33
34
35

PARTING IS "JUST" SORROW

1 *CAST:* Angie, Amy and Kay
2 *SETTING:* A pizza parlor — just a round table with a pizza box
3 *AT RISE:* The three girls are eating.
4
5 ANGIE: **Well, girls, this is the last time we have a pizza pigout.**
6 AMY: **Not the last. Kay will come back to visit and we'll go**
7 **see her this summer.**
8 KAY: **Chicago is a long way from Colorado Springs, Amy.**
9 **Your folks will never let you come to see me.**
10 AMY: **Sure they will. We'll hold our breath, pout, refuse to**
11 **eat our veggies.**
12 ANGIE: **Those tactics haven't worked since we were seven.**
13 KAY: **I'm going to hate my new school. I'll be a misfit — new**
14 **kid. You know how we treated new kids in school.**
15 ANGIE: **We were nice to Kim.**
16 AMY: **Not really.**
17 KAY: **Making her do our homework, fetch our silverware and**
18 **polish our shoes just so she could sit at our lunch table**
19 **was hardly considered an act of kindness!**
20 AMY: **Well, you're cute, Kay. You'll be running around with**
21 **the "in" group in three days.**
22 ANGIE: **Yeah, your social life will be so full, you won't have**
23 **time to write or call.**
24 KAY: **Oh, sure. All the misfits will hit on me and I'll probably**
25 **be tattooed and initiated into a gang.**
26 ANGIE: **You'll be fine, Kay. We're the ones who won't recover.**
27 AMY: **I can't believe it: the Terrible Trio breaking up!**
28 KAY: **I know. We've been together since second grade — sat**
29 **together . . . same dance lessons, Brownie troop, ortho-**
30 **dontist, dermatologist, cosmetologist . . . Oh my gosh,**
31 **who'll cut my hair?! Nobody but Anne has touched our**
32 **hair since we played beauty operator and gave each other**
33 **Mohawkette hair cuts.**

1 ANGIE: They'll have stylists in Chicago. You'll look great!
2 KAY: Then there's Kyle. We were just developing a
3 relationship. I worked so hard to get him to notice me.
4 AMY: Kyle will keep in touch. He's one of the good guys.
5 ANGIE: We'll throw rocks at him if we see him eyeing any
6 other girl.
7 KAY: No, we broke it off . . . can't go steady that far apart.
8 It's going to take a long time for me to forgive my father
9 for ripping my life apart like this.
10 ANGIE: He's not at the top of our list either.
11 AMY: Speaking of your father . . .
12 KAY: Oh, no . . . my dad's out there. I guess this is good-bye.
13 We're leaving early in the morning. *(All hug.)* I'm never
14 going to forget you. We'll always be best friends . . . promise?
15 ANGIE/AMY: We promise.
16 ANGIE: Write every week.
17 AMY: And call.
18 KAY: And Dad promised I could go to Colorado State with
19 you . . . roommates, sorority sisters — Tri Sigs forever,
20 right?
21 ANGIE/AMY: Right.
22 KAY: I hate my dad for taking me away from my hometown,
23 my high school and my friends. But I shall return. Just
24 don't forget me. *(Exits.)*
25 ANGIE: We've lost our best friend.
26 AMY: It'll never be the same. Letters and phone calls just
27 won't get it.
28 ANGIE: She'll have a new best friend in a week.
29 AMY: Let's go. I've lost my appetite.
30 ANGIE: Me, too, but we'll get it back. But we won't get our
31 friend Kay back.
32
33
34
35

55

THE LINE-UP

1 *CAST:* Caleb, James, Barney and Ms. Sharptooth
2 *SETTING:* Principal's office
3 *AT RISE:* The three culprits come into the office as the scene opens.
4 Ms. Sharptooth is sitting at her desk, shining a set of handcuffs,
5 polishing a knife and cleaning a gun.
6
7 **SHARPTOOTH: Well, don't just stand there. Come on in.**
8 **You're letting out all of the air conditioning, and some of**
9 **it might find its way down to a classroom. Can't have that!**
10 **We need to meet our quota of heat stroke victims.** *(Boys*
11 *come in. She walks around them, eyeing each suspiciously.)* **Well,**
12 **well, well . . . you're here, so you may as well sit**
13 **down . . . down, down, down! Now, give me your discipline**
14 **referral slips. Let's see what you're in for.** *(Each hands her*
15 *a paper. To JAMES)* **So, it's Jesse James, is it, on the loose**
16 **again? Robbing from the rich and keeping it for your** ***poor***
17 **little self, huh James?**
18 **JAMES: I didn't mean to take their money. I just went back**
19 **to the locker room to get a Kleenex. I got a nose bleed**
20 **playing basketball.**
21 **SHARPTOOTH: And I suppose all the loose change from**
22 **everyone's pockets just jumped into your greedy little**
23 **mitts, huh? Huh?**
24 **JAMES: Kind of. It was like a magnet pulling me towards**
25 **everyone's billfolds, change, watches. I was under some**
26 **kind of spell.**
27 **SHARPTOOTH: Well, Mr. Nomercy will break the curse. He'll**
28 **ex-*spell* you!** *(Laughs hysterically.)*
29 **CALEB: Hey, don't try to scare him. He's new at this. It's his**
30 **first offense.**
31 **SHARPTOOTH: While you, Caleb, are here so often you have**
32 **your own chair.**
33 **CALEB: Yep. Brought me a special pillow . . . got tired of that**

1 **hard wood.**
2 **SHARPTOOTH: You'll think hard wood. Did you know the**
3 **school board at a special meeting last night reinstated**
4 **corporal punishment?** *(The boys gasp.)* **Yes, gentlemen, the**
5 **paddle's back . . . or a few inches *down* from your back.**
6 *(Laughs hysterically.)* **I do so love my work! And they tried**
7 **to get caning — came out a three to four vote. Maybe next**
8 **month when we get a new board.**
9 **CALEB: You mean Mr. Nomercy is in there right now with a**
10 **big paddle, beating kids' buns?** *(They hear loud hitting*
11 *sounds and yelling Off-stage. All look scared.)*
12 **BARNEY: Was that what I thought it was?**
13 **SHARPTOOTH: He's just warming up his right arm on a**
14 **couple of tardies. He'll get his swing back. They used to**
15 **call him The Crusher.** *(More yelling is heard.)*
16 **JAMES: I want my mommy!**
17 **SHARPTOOTH: Yep, old Jesse James was a mama's boy, too.**
18 **CALEB: I want to see my lawyer.**
19 **BARNEY: Don't we get one phone call?**
20 **SHARPTOOTH: You have no rights. You gave them all up**
21 **when you** *(Looking at discipline referral papers)* **stole personal**
22 **belongings,** *(Gives JAMES a cold stare)* **visited the girls'**
23 **restroom** *(Gives BARNEY the evil eye)* **and called Mr.**
24 **Wordsworth a blathering idiot** *(Is eyeball to eyeball with*
25 *CALEB)*.
26 **CALEB: Well, it's true. Have you ever sat in on one of**
27 **Wordyword's lectures . . . when he gets all revved up about**
28 **Shakespeare or Keats or Shelly? He never lets up. He just**
29 **keeps going and going and going and going. I was**
30 **beginning to fear for his mind! It wasn't an act of**
31 **disrespect; it was an act of mercy. I got a standing ovation**
32 **from the class!**
33 **SHARPTOOTH: I suspect you'll be doing some standing**
34 **yourself when Mr. Nomercy gets done with you.**
35 **CALEB: It's not fair. A guy tries to perform a humanitarian**

1 service, and does he get rewarded? No. Bet the Good
2 Samaritan didn't get his butt beat when he tried to help
3 out.
4 SHARPTOOTH: The Good Samaritan probably didn't have
5 fifty-six other discipline referrals for this year. *(Holds up*
6 *thick file.)*
7 JAMES: But my file is clean until today. Surely I'll get
8 probation, not the paddle!
9 SHARPTOOTH: I don't know. Stealing really rubs Nomercy
10 the wrong way . . . ever since somebody stole his shoes
11 while he was taking a shower at the gym where he works
12 out. He had to walk home on hot sidewalk.
13 CALEB: Nomercy *works out*? And his body still looks like the
14 Good Year . . . *(Sees SHARPTOOTH's face.)* Oh, sorry. I just
15 got carried away . . . was so impressed with our esteemed
16 principal's attempt to set a good example for us by leading
17 the way to good health through proper exercise.
18 SHARPTOOTH: Can it! Now you, Barney. What do you have
19 to say for yourself? What excuse do you have for your visit
20 to the little girls' room?
21 CALEB: I think somebody shoved him in, isn't that right,
22 Barney? It was some big guy. He didn't catch his face.
23 SHARPTOOTH: I'm going to catch *your* face, Caleb, in a head-
24 lock. I work out, too! *(CALEB laughs, makes fun behind her*
25 *back over this remark. She turns and almost catches him.)* Now,
26 what's the story, Barney?
27 BARNEY: *(Timidly)* It was my glasses. They were all fogged
28 over. I couldn't read the sign over the door.
29 CALEB: And he is in a special reading class. *(Cold stare from*
30 *SHARPTOOTH)*
31 SHARPTOOTH: Don't think Nomercy will buy that bag of
32 garbage. You've been in this building for three years. You
33 should know where the johns are.
34 JAMES: Tell her the truth, Barney. It's no shame. He needed
35 to get to a bathroom fast, and the girls' was closer.

1 **SHARPTOOTH: Uh-huh . . .**
2 **CALEB: And he wanted to get some change from that machine**
3 **on the wall.**
4 **SHARPTOOTH: Let's see what we've got here: a fifty-time**
5 **loser** *(Pointing to CALEB, who stands and bows)*, **a pervert**
6 *(Looking at BARNEY)* **and a member of the James gang. I**
7 **think Nomercy is going to have a good morning! He'll**
8 **really enjoy getting his swatting arm back on the likes of**
9 **you. Let me go see if he's ready to hear your pitiful stories.**
10 *(Exits.)*
11 **BARNEY: I'm really scared. Maybe if I throw myself at his**
12 **feet, hang onto his legs, cry my guts out and promise to**
13 **never go to any bathroom again . . .**
14 **CALEB: Man, that won't work. By the way, why** ***did*** **you go**
15 **in there? Even a pro like myself knows better than that.**
16 **BARNEY: I just wanted to look around. You know how**
17 **everybody always says girls have more graffiti on the walls**
18 **and keep their restrooms filthy. That's why Nomercy has**
19 **to keep taking the outside door off the girls' restrooms. I**
20 **wanted to see for myself . . . inquiring minds, you know!**
21 **JAMES: Well?**
22 **CALEB: Yeah, out with it. Are girls really pigs?**
23 **BARNEY: I never saw anything like it . . . cigarette butts**
24 **everywhere, stools unflushed, graffiti all over the walls. It**
25 **was totally digusting!**
26 **CALEB: I suppose my name and phone number were up there**
27 **in bold letters!**
28 **BARNEY: I didn't have time to read much, although there**
29 **was some X-rated poetry about some guy; but before I**
30 **could read it all, Mr. Wordsworth grabbed me by the ear**
31 **and marched me down here. I didn't even get time to wash**
32 **my hands . . . not that I would have touched anything in**
33 **that restroom!**
34 **JAMES: I've got a great idea. Why don't you write an article**
35 **about the girls' restrooms for the next issue of the school**

1 **paper. I'm on the staff, and that would make interesting**
2 **reading.**
3 **BARNEY: I'd be glad to . . . sort of an insider's view, huh?**
4 **JAMES: Oh, no, here comes Ms. Sharptooth, and she's**
5 **grinning.**
6 **CALEB: That's no grin . . . that's a smirk!**
7 **BARNEY: Is Mr. Nomercy as awful as they say?**
8 **CALEB: Oh, he's not so bad. We're on a first-name basis. Of**
9 **course, he sees me more often than he does his barber.**
10 **JAMES: Do you think he'll really expel me . . . just for helping**
11 **myself to everybody's money and stuff?**
12 **CALEB: Can't say for sure . . . kinda depends on his mood.**
13 **Some days he's OK . . . will listen to reason. Other days**
14 **he's mean and does whatever Sharptooth recommends. I**
15 **think he needs more fiber in his diet.**
16 **BARNEY: I'd be glad to bring him a box of All-Bran if he'd**
17 **just go easy on me!**
18 **JAMES: Do they always call your folks when you're brought**
19 **to the office?**
20 **CALEB: I'm afraid so. My dad had a direct line put in to**
21 **Nomercy's office.**
22 **BARNEY: My mother will die. She'll think I've smeared the**
23 **family name. Grandma will take me out of the will. Uncle**
24 **Bernie won't want me to come into his law firm.**
25 **JAMES: My dad will beat my butt a lot harder than Nomercy**
26 **does. I'll be sitting on pillows tomorrow.**
27 **CALEB: Well, she's motioning for us to come in. Let's be *men.***
28 **JAMES: OK, a man's gotta do . . .**
29 **BARNEY: Be brave . . . be brave . . . be brave . . . don't cry . . .**
30 **don't beg . . .**
31 **CALEB: Let's go face the music, men.** *(Stands back, letting the*
32 *others go first.)* **After you, gentlemen. After all, for me this**
33 **is just a rerun!**
34
35

56

BEAUTY SLEEP

1 *CAST:* Beth, Linda, Adrianne, Patti, Kisa and Margo
2 *SETTING:* Beth's bedroom. The floor is covered with sleeping bags.
3 *AT RISE:* The girls are sprawled all over the floor in their pajamas.
4
5 **LINDA: I'm so glad you're having this last slumber party for**
6 **us, Beth . . . can't believe we'll be graduating next week.**
7 **BETH:** *(Grabbing her graduation hat and humming "Pomp and*
8 *Circumstance," she marches around.)* **It'll feel great to be out**
9 **of school.**
10 **MARGO: Of course, we'll all be off to different colleges in**
11 **August.**
12 **KISA: I wish one of you would change your mind and come**
13 **to the University with me.**
14 **ADRIANNE: Oh, don't be such a scaredy cat, Kisa. It'll do**
15 **you good to be on your own. You've been too protected**
16 **by your folks.**
17 **KISA: Look who's talking . . . and look who's going to be**
18 **living with her grandmother!**
19 **ADRIANNE: Just until I save a little more money . . . and**
20 **Grams only lives two blocks from campus, and she has a**
21 **whole empty basement, with an outside entrance.**
22 **PATTI: Sounds smart to me. Wish I had a grandma. It costs**
23 **a bunch to stay at a dorm nowadays.**
24 **BETH: Well, I'm moving into the sorority house as soon as I**
25 **can. That's where all the action is.**
26 **LINDA: I don't think I'll pledge my first year . . . want to give**
27 **my studies a fair shake.**
28 **MARGO: Leave it to Linda to want to go to college to study!**
29 **LINDA: What's wrong with that? Why are the rest of you**
30 **going?**
31 **ALL BUT LINDA:** ***Guys!***
32 **BETH: Frat rats . . .**
33 **PATTI: Football jocks . . .**

1 **MARGO: Guys studying to be doctors . . .**
2 **ADRIANNE: Studs with I.Q.s . . .**
3 **KISA: Guys with cool cars and money . . .**
4 **LINDA: Listen to yourselves. We're all liberated women with**
5 **futures for ourselves. We don't need guys to give us**
6 **identities.**
7 **MARGO: We're not looking for identity. We're looking for fun!**
8 **KISA: That's why most girls go to college.**
9 **LINDA: That's why they used to go to college, but those days**
10 **are over. Now they go for the opportunities.**
11 **ADRIANNE: Opportunities . . . that's what we're talking**
12 **about here. Opportunity to meet more good-looking guys**
13 **than we've ever seen in this one-horse town!**
14 **BETH: Opportunity to fill out little black books to the brim!**
15 **PATTI: I can't wait. I may enroll in summer school.**
16 **MARGO: They say that's a mistake. None of the cool bunch**
17 **go to summer school . . . just a bunch of teachers renewing**
18 **their teaching certificates.**
19 **KISA: That's all I'd need . . . be in a class with some of my old**
20 **teachers.**
21 **ADRIANNE: That's one of the reasons we want to get out of**
22 **this town.**
23 **PATTI: And our boring lives.**
24 **LINDA: Now, come on. It hasn't been all that boring. The six**
25 **of us have always had a good time.**
26 **ADRIANNE: That's true. Ever since third grade when we**
27 **ended up in the same reading group, we've stuck together.**
28 **KISA: Through thick and thin. I'm talking about our bodies**
29 **here.**
30 **BETH: She's talking about all those crazy diets she put us on!**
31 **LINDA: Uh, the worst was the one where we ate bananas one**
32 **day, eggs the next . . .**
33 **MARGO: Raw carrots till our tongues turned orange . . .**
34 **PATTI: And we all gained three pounds!**
35 **KISA: I still say you were all cheating . . . had Snickers in your**

1 pillowcases.
2 ADRIANNE: Think of all the different clubs we organized
3 through the years.
4 BETH: There was the We Hate Boys Club. It was very popular
5 in fifth grade.
6 PATTI: The boys in our class were so bad, Ms. Palmer, our
7 teacher, wanted to join!
8 LINDA: Then there was the Weird Hairdo Club in ninth grade.
9 Do you remember how we all looked in our freshman
10 pictures?
11 KISA: Who could forget? Adrianne had her hair dyed "Lucy"
12 red, Margo wore pigtails, Linda had Shirley Temple curls
13 bouncing around on her head, Patti had that bleached
14 streak down the back like Pepy LaPew, and Beth went
15 bouffant — her head was the size of a watermelon!
16 PATTI: And you, Kisa, shaved one side of your head. It's a
17 wonder our mothers didn't disown us.
18 ADRIANNE: They just kept saying it was a phase we were
19 going through.
20 MARGO: As sophomores we organized the Ban the
21 Lunchroom Club. We brown bagged it all that year. To
22 this day I can't look a peanut butter sandwich in the eye.
23 KISA: Yeah, even school lunch tasted good after that.
24 PATTI: I think the worst club was last year: the Going Steady
25 Club.
26 LINDA: That was all your fault, Kisa.
27 KISA: I just thought it was a clever idea.
28 BETH: Clever? I went with that dorky Henry for five months
29 just so I could stay in your stupid club.
30 ADRIANNE: Me, too, and Sammy still follows me around and
31 sends me poetry saying how we're soul mates.
32 MARGO: That's right. Kisa forced the rest of us into going
33 with jerks, just so we wouldn't be left out of her silly club.
34 KISA: Well, it worked, and you probably all learned
35 something from the experience.

1 **LINDA: Yes, we learned to ignore your scatterbrained clubs.**
2 **KISA: See, I taught you all something valuable.**
3 **MARGO: And we learned to beware of nerds.**
4 **ADRIANNE: Especially ones writing poetry.**
5 **PATTI: Do you know what I'm afraid of? I'm afraid we'll all**
6 **go our separate ways and forget each other after all these**
7 **years together being friends.**
8 **LINDA: No way that could happen . . . we're all too close.**
9 **KISA: Right. We know each other's secrets!**
10 **MARGO: We'll always stay in touch . . . like sisters.**
11 **BETH: Better than sisters . . . we all like each other!**
12 **ADRIANNE: We've been through too much together. We *are***
13 **each other's childhood.**
14 **PATTI: But we could forget and just see each other at class**
15 **reunions.**
16 **LINDA: We'll all be home for holidays and summer vacations.**
17 **BETH: Nothing's going to split up this bunch!**
18 **KISA: Let's make a pact, right now.**
19 **ALL: Oh, no . . .**
20 **KISA: Now just listen . . . we'll make a pact to contact each**
21 **other by letter or phone once a month. Agreed?**
22 **MARGO: What if we get busy and forget?**
23 **KISA: We'll need some sort of penalty.**
24 **ALL: Oh, no . . .**
25 **KISA: Now, nothing like when we used to do the splinters**
26 **under the fingernails or let the ants bite the guilty one.**
27 **OK, OK, no putting heads in the toilets and flushing.**
28 **PATTI: Maybe we're mature enough. Maybe we don't need a**
29 **penalty.**
30 **LINDA: Let's just put everyone on the honor system.**
31 **ADRIANNE: Are we really ready for that?**
32 **BETH: If we're ready for college, we're ready to be trusted**
33 **completely.**
34 **KISA: Agreed. We keep in touch each month or else . . .**
35 **LINDA: Or else we don't.**

PATTI: **But it's still scary . . . graduating, leaving home, missing your family and friends.**

BETH: **I think that's what growing up's all about.**

ADRIANNE: **You don't often think about the sad part . . . the good-byes.**

KISA: **But not this bunch. We all have AT&T cards.**

LINDA: **Right, we can "reach out and touch" anytime we want.**

PATTI: **And we'll meet on weekends and invite each other to special events at our schools.**

BETH: *(Handing each a Pepsi)* **Let's make a toast** *(Holding up her can)* **to the six best friends . . . long may they stick together!**

MARGO: *(Holding up her can)* **To us . . . may our futures be bright and as much fun as our pasts.**

LINDA: *(Holding up can)* **May we stay in each other's minds, hearts and prayers.**

ADRIANNE: *(Raising can)* **May we each reach our goals in life and help each other along the way.**

PATTI: *(Lifting can)* **Make new friends, but keep the old. And you guys are all pure gold.**

KISA: *(Last to lift can)* **To us . . . the six best females this town has ever known. We're sure to leave our echo here when we move on to our institutions of higher learning. May we all find the guy of our dreams, follow our hearts and find success in whatever path we choose to follow. Here's to us.** *(They all touch cans, drink, then hug and gossip. Or, if you wish a lighter ending and the janitor is on vacation, let them spray the Pepsis on each other and laugh and giggle.)*

OLD MAIDS' CLUB

1 *CAST:* Bev, Tootie, Chris and Stacey
2 *SETTING:* Local teenage fast food place. A table and four chairs
3 are needed.
4 *AT RISE:* Three girls are seated. Bev is standing, calling the
5 meeting to order.
6
7 **BEV: The meeting of the Old Maids' Club will now come to**
8 **order. Chris, read the minutes from the last meeting.** *(Sits.)*
9 **CHRIS:** *(Stands and reads.)* **The meeting of the Old Maids' Club**
10 **took place last month in the Pizza Shack. Roll was**
11 **answered by telling some insensitive, obnoxious thing a**
12 **guy had done or said to us during the week. Stacey won**
13 **the coveted Old Maids' Manual with her story of her steady**
14 **boyfriend, Ted, taking her twin sister, Tracy, line dancing**
15 **while she had the chicken pox. The group exchanged other**
16 **"gruesome guy" stories over pepperoni pizza. The meeting**
17 **adjourned.** *(Sits.)*
18 **BEV: Any corrections or additions?**
19 **TOOTIE: Take a look at that cute guy over there!** *(Points to*
20 *Off-stage Right.)*
21 **CHRIS: Tootie, you know we aren't allowed to look at guys**
22 **during an official meeting.**
23 **TOOTIE: Oops!**
24 **STACEY: No corrections or additions, Madame President.**
25 **BEV: Then they stand approved as read. Tootie, remember**
26 **our motto:**
27 **ALL:** *(Stand and say.)* **Guys will cheat on you, they belong in**
28 **jails. Remember, they're made from puppy dog tails!**
29 **TOOTIE: But puppies have such *cute* tails.**
30 **ALL BUT TOOTIE: Tootie!**
31 **TOOTIE: Sorry, but look at those eyes . . . and biceps that**
32 **belong on magazine covers.**
33 **BEV: But what do we know from past experience about guys,**

1 **Tootie?**
2 **TOOTIE: That they lie, cheat and say whatever it takes to**
3 **make a girl melt in their arms . . . but take a look at those**
4 **arms!**
5 **CHRIS: That does it. Trade seats with me, Tootie. You're too**
6 **distracted.** *(They trade seats. CHRIS faces Stage Right.)*
7 **BEV: Now, Stacey, it's time for roll call.**
8 **STACEY:** *(Standing)* **Yes, today's roll will be answered by two**
9 **disgustingly chauvinistic words from our dictionary.**
10 **Playing up the male gender, Mr. Webster, like so many**
11 **other males before and after him, shortchanged the female**
12 **population. Now, our words highlighting that it's a *man's***
13 **world . . . my own contributions are: sports*man*ship and**
14 ***man*ners.** *(All clap.)* **Chris?**
15 **CHRIS: Wow, he *is* good looking. I think he winked at me!**
16 **STACEY: Get over here, Chris. You're as boy crazy as Tootie!**
17 *(They trade places.)*
18 **TOOTIE: Hey!**
19 **STACEY: Now, Chris, let's have your two man words.**
20 **CHRIS: Oh, yes . . . *Mayon*naise and *man*ager.** *(All clap.)*
21 **STACEY: Good. Now, Tootie, it's your turn.**
22 **TOOTIE: Oh, goody. I've really been giving this a lot of**
23 **thought. *Man*nequin and *man* hungry.** *(All clap hesitantly.)*
24 **STACEY: Ummm . . . man hungry . . . man hungry . . . You**
25 **know, that guy is without a doubt the best-looking thing**
26 **I've seen since I saw a Tom Cruise/Mel Gibson double**
27 **feature.**
28 **BEV: Oh, for heaven's sake. Are you all falling apart? Let me**
29 **sit there. I'm the only strong one in the bunch. I don't**
30 **know how the three of you stay members of the Old Maids'**
31 **Club!** *(Trades places with STACEY.)* **And by the way, my**
32 **man words are *man*iac and *man*ure.** *(All clap loudly.)*
33 **TOOTIE: You win, Bev. You had the best words. I don't know**
34 **how you *man*aged!**
35 **STACEY: It's your turn to keep the Old Maids' *Man*ual.** *(Hands*

1 *it to her.)*
2 **CHRIS: As *man*dated by our by-laws, we must close the**
3 **meeting after the *man*ual presentation.**
4 **BEV: Thanks for this book; I'll put it on my *man*tle. Now, I**
5 **suggest that we go by that stud muffin's table on our way**
6 **out. He's some piece of work! The meeting of the Old Maids'**
7 **Club is definitely adjourned!**
8
9
10
11
12
13
14
15
16
17
18
19
20
21
22
23
24
25
26
27
28
29
30
31
32
33
34
35

58

DO UNTO OTHERS

1 *CAST:* Five teenage girls
2 *SETTING:* Study hall
3 *AT RISE:* The girls are gathered around a table arguing.
4
5 GIRL #1: **I still say we should do our senior community project**
6 **on updating the girls' dressing room behind the stage. It's**
7 **the pits.**
8 GIRL #2: **It's just because you're a drama major and had the**
9 **lead in all the school plays. That dressing room isn't used**
10 **all that often.**
11 GIRL #1: **Do you have a better idea for our community**
12 **project?**
13 GIRL #3: **I think it's terrible they added this community**
14 **service clause to our diploma . . . no community service,**
15 **no diploma.**
16 GIRL #4: **They're trying to turn us all into little Florence**
17 **Nightingales, and it won't work!**
18 GIRL #5: **I think it's a good idea. Kids graduate without a**
19 **sense of community.**
20 GIRL #1: **Well, it doesn't matter if we like doing it or not.**
21 **We've got to do it.**
22 GIRL #2: **And we've got to do it cooperatively . . . work**
23 **together for the good of all.**
24 GIRL #3: **The only good thing is that we'll graduate.**
25 GIRL #5: **Maybe we can do something worthwhile . . .**
26 **something that might make a difference.**
27 GIRL #4: **Like what?**
28 GIRL #5: **Oh, we could help out at nursing homes, shelters**
29 **for battered wives, Salvation Army.**
30 GIRL #3: **That sounds like a thrill a minute.**
31 GIRL #5: **We're not supposed to be doing this for us. That's**
32 **the whole idea.**
33 GIRL #2: **OK, who do we know that needs help?**

1 **GIRL #4: Every guy I know needs help . . . mental help!**
2 **GIRL #2: We don't have enough resources to tackle a project**
3 **that big!**
4 **GIRL #1: Well, that new girl in homeroom . . . Jessica . . . I**
5 **heard the counselor telling Ms. Burk that her family's**
6 **home burned down. There are five children and no father.**
7 **GIRL #2: Wow. I know Jessica; she's in my gym class.**
8 **GIRL #4: How could we take on a project like that?**
9 **GIRL #5: Easy. We get Ms. Burk to help us. We find out the**
10 **ages of the children, get clothes and food, and raise money**
11 **for them.**
12 **GIRL #3: Wouldn't that be embarrassing for Jessica, to know**
13 **her classmates were providing charity to her family?**
14 **GIRL #5: She won't have to know where the help came from.**
15 **That's the best part of the project. The workers remain**
16 **anonymous.**
17 **GIRL #3: You mean we do all that work and don't get any**
18 **thanks or credit?**
19 **GIRL #4: You'll get your community credit that you need for**
20 **graduation.**
21 **GIRL #1: And I guess the best part of doing something for**
22 **somebody is the *doing* . . . not being thanked for doing it.**
23 **GIRL #5: Now that's it exactly. Let's take a vote: how many**
24 **in favor of helping Jessica's family for our community**
25 **project?** *(All hands go up slowly. GIRL #3 is the last to raise.)*
26 **GIRL #1: Let's meet back here tomorrow at this time. I'll see**
27 **if Ms. Burk will join us.**
28 **GIRL #2: I'll check with the counselor and find out the ages**
29 **and clothing sizes of the children.**
30 **GIRL #4: I'll talk to my mom about ways to raise money for**
31 **needy causes. She's always helping at the church.**
32 **GIRL #5: That's great. Let's all think about this tonight and**
33 **make lists of all the things we can do to help.**
34 **GIRL #3: I'll go by the office and get our community project**
35 **forms. If we *must* do this, we sure want the credit.**

1 **GIRL #5: Good idea. Now, anything else? I might suggest that**
2 **we keep a lid on our project. We don't want to cause any**
3 **embarrassment for Jessica.**
4 **GIRL #2: I think we're all going to be getting something out**
5 **of this. It was a good idea.**
6 **GIRL #5: I think we'll be helping Jessica and her family, but**
7 **when it's all over, I think we'll be the big winners.** *(Gathers*
8 *up books as curtain falls.)*
9
10
11
12
13
14
15
16
17
18
19
20
21
22
23
24
25
26
27
28
29
30
31
32
33
34
35

59

PARTY TIME

1 *CAST:* Julie, Stan, Tom and Ben
2 *SETTING:* Front room of Tom's house
3 *AT RISE:* All four teenagers are sweeping and picking up. The
4 room is a mess.
5
6 **JULIE: I can't believe what they did to this house.**
7 **STAN: It doesn't take long for a houseful of teenagers to tear**
8 **a place apart.**
9 **TOM: I'm just glad we had a little time to clean up before my**
10 **parents get here.**
11 **BEN: What will you tell your folks, Tom?**
12 **STAN: Yeah. You're gonna be grounded till you're as old as**
13 **Colonel Sanders.**
14 **TOM: I'm a dead man. Mom reminded me over and over: *no***
15 **party while they're gone.**
16 **BEN: But did she really *mean* it?**
17 **TOM: Dad put me on my honor.**
18 **STAN: Wow, that makes it tough!**
19 **JULIE: It's partly you guys' fault. You kept telling everyone,**
20 **inviting the world.**
21 **BEN: Not true. You know how unpopular Stan and I are. We**
22 **don't know very many people.**
23 **STAN: And most of the people we do know are nerds . . . kids**
24 **who think going to TCBY is having a high old time . . . not**
25 **that wild bunch that was here tonight.**
26 **BEN: Yeah. Where did they all come from?**
27 **JULIE: The three with tattoos were sure sweethearts!**
28 **STAN: And I guess black leather jackets are making a**
29 **comeback.**
30 **TOM: I didn't know half of them myself.**
31 **BEN: They weren't even from our school.**
32 **STAN: A lot of them couldn't even spell school.**
33 **JULIE: Well, the word got spread somehow.**

1 **STAN: I saw it on the news bulletin at school.**
2 **TOM: What?**
3 **BEN: We thought you put it there, you know, to save calling**
4 **people.**
5 **JULIE: The journalism class did show up for a while . . . until**
6 **the fight broke out.**
7 **STAN: And I think they learned which is mightier — the pen**
8 **or a seven-inch blade!**
9 **TOM: Well, I sure wish I'd enjoyed the party. It's the last one**
10 **I'll attend till my own "over the hill" party.**
11 **JULIE: Maybe your folks will be more understanding than**
12 **you think.**
13 **TOM:** *(Holding up some broken object)* **Fat chance!**
14 **STAN: I don't know, your folks are pretty cool.**
15 **BEN: Yeah. They treat you like an adult, not some demented**
16 **teenager.**
17 **TOM: That was *before* this episode.**
18 **JULIE: It wasn't all your fault, Tom. You only invited a**
19 **handful of your best friends — good kids — but then**
20 **somehow it just snowballed.**
21 **BEN: It doesn't take long for word to get around about free**
22 **food.**
23 **STAN: And drinks.**
24 **JULIE: Tom didn't have any alcoholic beverages.**
25 **BEN: Tom didn't, but some of his uninvited guests sure did.**
26 **TOM: Oh, it's still all my fault . . . and when Granddad came**
27 **. . . and the police . . .**
28 **JULIE: Your folks will understand and forgive you. They're**
29 **good people.**
30 **TOM: Oh, they'll forgive me and still love me. I have super**
31 **parents. But it'll be a long time before they *trust* me again.**
32 **STAN: And your mom might be ticked about the broken stuff.**
33 **BEN: And the stains.**
34 **JULIE: It would have been worse if the neighbors hadn't**
35 **called the cops.**

1 **TOM:** Well, it's over. We've cleaned up all we can. Thanks,
2 guys.
3 **BEN:** No problem. Do you want us to hang around?
4 **STAN:** Yeah, do you need back-up when your folks get here?
5 **JULIE:** We can explain how it wasn't all your fault.
6 **TOM:** No. I'm going to have to face this on my own. I broke
7 a promise I made. I'm going to have to suffer the
8 consequences . . . and my dad's great with consequences.
9 He'll come up with a perfect punishment — one that fits
10 the crime.
11 **STAN:** Well, he is a criminal lawyer!
12 **BEN:** Let us know the verdict . . . and the sentence.
13 **JULIE:** Give us a call.
14 **STAN:** Unless you lose phone privileges.
15 **JULIE:** Are you sure you don't need us?
16 **TOM:** I'm sure. Go on home. I need time to plan my defense.
17 **BEN:** Try throwing yourself on the mercy of the court.
18 **STAN:** I vote for crying and pleading and begging. Remind
19 them of what a cute baby you were . . . that you were an
20 altar boy . . . that you never take the Lord's name in vain.
21 **JULIE:** Come on, guys. Tom needs to think. He doesn't need
22 your harebrained ideas. If there's anything we can do,
23 Tom . . .
24 **TOM:** Thanks. I'll talk to you tomorrow. *(Three exit. TOM begins*
25 *to pace.)* Let's see . . . Mom, Dad, I know you're not going
26 to believe this . . . Nah! Dad, did you ever make a mistake?
27 Won't work . . . lawyers never make mistakes. Or they
28 don't admit them — just send them to jail! Now is no time
29 to try to be funny. OK, here goes again. I made a mistake,
30 it was stupid, I deserve to be punished. Yeah, that's better.
31 Uh-oh, here they are. Maybe the pleading and begging
32 wasn't such a bad idea. And here's my baby picture. I'll
33 set that out. They may want to use it to put in my obituary.
34 *(Curtain starts to close.)* Mom, Dad, I'm so glad you're
35 home . . .

60

OUT ON GOOD BEHAVIOR

1 ***CAST:*** Fifteen teenagers (male and female; #4 and #9 must be
2 male; #12 must be female). Mr. Johnny, principal.
3 ***SETTING:*** Detention room
4 ***AT RISE:*** Fifteen students are serving in-school suspension. They
5 are seated at desks.
6
7 #1: **Hey, where's Mr. Stout?**
8 #2: **I think he went to take a telephone message.**
9 #3: **You mean they left a bunch of convicts like us alone . . .**
10 **unsupervised?**
11 #4: **You'd think they'd be afraid we'd burn the place down.**
12 **Anybody gotta match?**
13 #5: **And you'd think they might be worried that we'd slip out**
14 **that back door. Is it locked?**
15 #6: **Oh, they know we aren't going anywhere. If we did, we'd**
16 **have our time doubled.**
17 #7: **Yeah, who wants to spend any more time out here than**
18 **they have to? This place is like a morgue.**
19 #8: **I like the peace and quiet. I can get my work done out**
20 **here without anybody bothering me.**
21 #9: **But there's no action out here . . . no excitement.**
22 #10: **Correct me if I'm wrong, but isn't it excitement that got**
23 **you here?**
24 #9: **Well, yes, but it's not my fault our principal has no sense**
25 **of humor . . . no taste . . . no flair!**
26 #11: **Flair . . . that's what you used to set off those firecrackers**
27 **in the lunchroom.**
28 #9: **Hey, everybody's always complaining that the food's cold!**
29 **Anybody for a little poker?** *(#13, #11 and #5 pull their desks*
30 *around and the four play cards as the scene progresses, throwing*
31 *a few coins around.)*
32 #12: **I can't believe it . . . gambling right here in school. If Mr.**
33 **Stout comes back and catches you, we'll all be in trouble,**

1 and I have had all the trouble I can take.
2 #13: What did a goody-goody like you do — forget to eat your
3 carrots?
4 #12: My offense is between me and my counselor.
5 #14: And your parole officer.
6 #15: And your defense attorney.
7 #1: Hey, maybe the school's on fire.
8 #2: And they just wanted to save Mr. Stout, not us.
9 #3: They probably figured one of us set it.
10 #4: No, we would have heard the fire bell. I'm an expert on
11 setting it off. It's kind of a hobby of mine.
12 #6: You're sort of a pyro-bell-maniac, huh?
13 #4: You could say that. I love to hear that constant beep, beep,
14 beep. It's music to my ears!
15 #5: I think you just do it because you like getting out of class
16 for fifteen minutes.
17 #4: It is true that I usually do my "bell" work in the afternoons
18 when I have science, math and English.
19 #7: Well, there's nobody outside. There's no smoke, so we can
20 forget about a fire.
21 #8: Be quiet. I'm trying to study. I wish Mr. Stout would get
22 back so we can have silence! And gambling is against my
23 religion.
24 #9: *(Mimicking #8)* "I wish Mr. Stout would get back." Are you
25 nuts? We get a little breather and this kid wants the warden
26 back.
27 #10: Hey, let's check Stout's desk . . . see if he has a math key.
28 #12: Stop. That's illegal, immoral and *soooo* wrong. We've
29 been put out here isolated from humanity to think about
30 our crimes, not to compound them. No rifling through Mr.
31 Stout's desk . . . understand?
32 #10: OK, OK, don't get your feathers up. But I don't see Billy
33 Graham looking in the window, do you?
34 #12: It doesn't matter. Somewhere, somebody knows!
35 #13: Wish somebody would step on Jiminy Cricket there.

1 #14: Hey, has anybody got the study questions done for
2 chapter eight in American history? I need to copy them.
3 #12: Didn't you hear a word I said? We're out here to
4 straighten up . . . overcome our vices . . .
5 #14: I'm trying to overcome that down letter I got in American
6 history so my old man will lift my grounding.
7 #11: I have the answers for chapter eight.
8 #14: But you got a flunk letter, too. Is there anybody here
9 who at least made a D? Is this room full of mush brains?
10 #15: I heard the counselor saying you were gifted. How can
11 somebody "gifted" be flunking all of his classes?
12 #14: It's easy. I don't give a flyin' flip about history . . . or
13 literature . . . or economics. I would like to spend the whole
14 day in the computer lab, but, *noooo*, I need a well-rounded
15 education. The only thing getting round is my butt, from
16 being parked in all of those stupid, sterile classrooms.
17 #1: I think something's really wrong. They might leave an
18 honors class unattended, but not the in-school suspension
19 room.
20 #2: I'm getting scared.
21 #3: I say we just sit back and enjoy the freedom.
22 #4: I think the school's being invaded by aliens. *(All except #8*
23 *and #12 make science fiction noises.)*
24 #12: That's not one bit funny. Maybe there's been some sort
25 of problem. Mr. Stout's too dedicated to forget about us.
26 #4: If the Martians come, can we all agree who is sent as a
27 lab specimen? *(All look at #12 and nod their heads.)*
28 #12: I think you need therapy.
29 #4: Well, for your information, I've had therapy.
30 #12: And?
31 #4: And it cost my old man big bucks. The therapist quit and
32 became a stockbroker, and I'm still the same happy-go-
33 lucky kid I always was!
34 #9: Somebody's always recommending I see a shrink, too.
35 #12: You should listen to good advice.

1 **#9: I will . . . when I hear some.**
2 **#6:** *(Standing at the window)* **Hey, Mr. Stout's out there, and**
3 **he's getting into his car.**
4 **#7: That does it. We've driven him bonkers!**
5 **#11: Well, it was just a matter of time.**
6 **#12: You should all be ashamed of yourselves. If Mr. Stout**
7 **has had a breakdown or quit his job, I'll hold you repeat**
8 **offenders personally responsible.**
9 **#4, #9, #14: What?**
10 **#12: You heard me. You could have straightened up, stayed**
11 **in class and given poor Mr. Stout some peace; but you**
12 **were too selfish . . . too pigheaded . . . too undisciplined.**
13 **#15:** *(Looking out door)* **Uh-oh. The principal's heading this**
14 **way. Everybody look busy.**
15 **#13: I am busy . . . drawing for a full house!**
16 **#8: I'd like to get busy if everybody would shut up so I could**
17 **concentrate. I'm glad we're getting supervision.**
18 **#9:** *(To* **#8) Do us all a favor, will you? Stay out of in-school**
19 **suspension. You give the place a bad name. You just don't**
20 **belong.**
21 **#12:** *(To* **#8) Consider that the best compliment you've ever**
22 **received. Only people like him and him** *(Points to #4 and*
23 *#9)* **and possibly him** *(Points to #14)* ***really*** **belong in a place**
24 **like this. The rest of you, wise up, shut up and grow up**
25 **so you don't have to be a prisoner again.**
26 **#15: You'd better break up the poker game. He's almost here.**
27 **#9: Maybe we can deal him in!**
28 **#12: For once, think of somebody besides yourself. Put the**
29 **cards away so we won't all get in trouble.**
30 **#4: Do it for us. If they gave all of us more days, guess who'd**
31 **be here** *(All look at #12)*, **and we wouldn't want anything**
32 **to stand in the way of her parole.** *(All agree.)*
33 **#12: Thanks for your support! And thank you all for putting**
34 **up the cards. Now, everybody look studious.**
35 **#1: Did she say stupid?**

1 **#2: Same thing as . . .**
2 **#3: *Heeerrreee's* Mr. Johnny!**
3 **MR. JOHNNY: Class, I see you've handled yourselves**
4 **admirably during Mr. Stout's absence. He said you would.**
5 **His wife just went into labor and he was needed at the**
6 **hospital. Since you've done such a remarkable job of**
7 **tending to business, I'm letting you go early . . . class**
8 **dismissed!** *(Cheers go up as STUDENTS [all but #9 and #12]*
9 *and MR. JOHNNY start to exit.)*
10 **#12: See, it does pay to do what's right.**
11 **#9: I'll say. I won seven bucks playing poker.**
12 **#12: I meant we were in our seats, being attentive, and Mr.**
13 **Johnny rewarded us for our behavior.**
14 **#9: And Lady Luck rewarded me with three aces and a pair**
15 **of jacks! Besides, I think he let us go because he was afraid**
16 **to stay shut up here with this many felons.**
17 **#12: He's a principal . . .**
18 **#9: And what do you think principals are? Teacher**
19 **rejects . . . ones that couldn't hack it at a chalkboard!**
20 **#12: You're hopeless.**
21 **#9: Are you going to be back here tomorrow?**
22 **#12: I'll never walk across this tainted threshold again.**
23 **#9: In English does that mean you've served your time?**
24 **#12: It most certainly does.**
25 **#9: Want to go have an ice cream cone with me . . . my treat?**
26 **#12: You're asking me out?**
27 **#9: It wasn't a proposal . . . just an invite for a double-dip ice**
28 **cream cone.**
29 **#12: Why would you possibly want to take *me* anywhere?**
30 **#9: Well, you look like you could use a snack . . . and you tried**
31 **to save this room full of lost souls today. Deeds like that**
32 **should be rewarded.**
33 **#12: I'm afraid nobody paid much attention to me.**
34 **#9: You never know . . . and besides, I think you're sorta**
35 **cute — in an up-tight sort of way.**

1 **#12: Me, cute?**
2 **#9: Well, you could be if you'd relax a little . . . not take life**
3 **and yourself so seriously!**
4 **#12: Well, I am rather goal oriented.**
5 **#9: Forget the vocabulary lesson. Let's treat our stomachs to**
6 **some Rocky Road.**
7 **#12: I really should go home and practice for my piano**
8 **recital . . . but I do like Rocky Road.**
9 **#9: Great, let's get out of this place.**
10 **#12: Are you back here tomorrow?**
11 **#9: Nope. I've served my time . . . and who knows, maybe**
12 **some of your good advice rubbed off on me. Maybe I just**
13 **needed the undying attention of a good woman. Maybe**
14 **because of your Joan of Arc attitude, I'll never return to**
15 **good old in-school suspension.** *(They exit.)*
16
17
18
19
20
21
22
23
24
25
26
27
28
29
30
31
32
33
34
35

ABOUT THE AUTHOR

Shirley Ullom keeps busy teaching speech/ drama in the Dodge City, Kansas school system, where she writes the plays her students perform.

Besides her teenage plays, Shirley has written humorous articles for *Country Woman, Woman Beautiful, Jest, Educational Oasis, Learning, The Dodge City Legend* and sold funny lines to Joan Rivers.

She is a member of the Kansas Authors Club, where she has won many writing contests/awards and has presented writing seminars.

NOTES

NOTES

Order Form

Meriwether Publishing Ltd.
PO Box 7710
Colorado Springs, CO 80933-7710
Phone: 800-937-5297 Fax: 719-594-9916
Website: www.meriwether.com

Please send me the following books:

________ **Get in the Act! #BK-B104** **$15.95**
by Shirley Ullom
Monologs, dialogs, and skits for teens

________ **Tough Acts to Follow #BK-B237** **$15.95**
by Shirley Ullom
75 monologs for teens

________ **Winning Monologs for Young Actors #BK-B127** **$15.95**
by Peg Kehret
Honest-to-life monologs for young actors

________ **Encore! More Winning Monologs for Young Actors #BK-B144** **$15.95**
by Peg Kehret
More honest-to-life monologs for young actors

________ **The Flip Side #BK-B221** **$15.95**
by Heather H. Henderson
64 point-of-view monologs for teens

________ **100 Great Monologs #BK-B276** **$15.95**
by Rebecca Young
A collection of monologs, duologs and triologs for actors

________ **Famous Fantasy Character Monologs #BK-B286** **$15.95**
by Rebecca Young
Starring the Not-So-Wicked Witch and more

These and other fine Meriwether Publishing books are available at your local bookstore or direct from the publisher. Prices subject to change without notice. Check our website or call for current prices.

Name: ________________________ e-mail: ________________________

Organization name: ____

Address: ____

City: ________________________________ State: ____________

Zip: ________________________ Phone: ________________________

❑ **Check enclosed**

❑ **Visa / MasterCard / Discover #** ____________________________

Signature: ____________________________ *Expiration date:* _______ / _______

(required for credit card orders)

Colorado residents: Please add 3% sales tax.
Shipping: Include $3.95 for the first book and 75¢ for each additional book ordered.

❑ *Please send me a copy of your complete catalog of books and plays.*